VENICE

JOHN KENT'S
VENICE

A Color Guide to the City

CHRONICLE BOOKS · SAN FRANCISCO

To Nina,
who says she prefers Florence

and with special thanks to
Michael Stephenson

First published in the United States in 1992 by Chronicle Books

First published 1988

Library of Congress Cataloging-in-Publication Data available

Cover design by Bradley Crouch

Printed in Italy

ISBN 0–8118–0131–4

1 3 5 7 9 10 8 6 4 2

Chronicle Books
275 Fifth Street
San Francisco, CA 94103

CONTENTS OF THE CITY

NOTE. Opening hours of museums and art galleries may vary from the times given; also, galleries are sometimes temporarily closed for restoration.

Venice began with refugees seeking sanctuary in the lagoon from the barbarian invasions of the 5th and 6th centuries. The first settlements were on the isle of Torcello, and at Malamocco on the Lido, where the first Doge (*Duca*) was elected in 726 as a declaration of independence from Byzantium. The momentous retreat to the present site in the centre of the lagoon was forced when Pepin, son of Charlemagne, attempted to invade in 810. Twenty years later, when the body of the apostle St Mark arrived from Alexandria, the new city found itself with the most prestigious patron saint outside of Rome. Both he and his emblem, the lion, were enthusiastically adopted as symbols of the city, and its independence.

If the lagoon was to protect Venice from foreign invasion for nearly 1,000 years, the constitution, limiting the power of the Doge, was to protect the city from internal conflict.

Rovigno
Pola
Zara
Sebenico
Ragusa
Cattaro
Scutari
Corfu
Cephalonia
Zante
More
Modon

Venice suffered neither the civil wars nor the tyrannies that afflicted other Italian cities. The citizens of the Serene Republic were free to concentrate their energies on commerce, which they did with great diligence in trade with the east. So successful were they, that by 1171 the Byzantine emperor, Manuel Comnenus, ordered the imprisonment of all Venetians in the empire, because of their stranglehold on its economy. This act led to the ignominious 4th Crusade, in which the Venetians extracted their revenge by diverting an invasion force from the Holy Land to the sack of Constantinople in 1204. The trading posts were now an empire, and for the next three centuries, Venice, at the height of its power, controlled the west's trade in luxuries and spices. Yet by 1508, when in anger and envy the rest of the western world turned on Venice (they failed at the lagoon), the seeds of decline had already been sown. Constantinople had been taken by the Turks, the Portuguese had discovered a route to India that bypassed the Rialto, and the Spanish had discovered America. Venice's *raison d'être* was slipping away.

As military power waned with the loss of earnings, so the great displays of power, the spectacles, grew. By the 18thC Venice had become a beautiful sham, and the one person to see it was Napoleon. 'I shall be an Attila to the state of Venice,' he said. And on 12 May 1797 he was.

plia

Crete

Cyprus

CUCINA VENEZIANA

'Venetians do not know how to eat or drink,' proclaimed Pietro Aretino in the 16thC. Their houses did not even have a dining-room, as such. Although they traded in rare spices, salt, pepper and sugar, the food they ate was, and remains, simple.

A cuisine is determined by the ingredients at hand, and the most common to be stirred into the Venetian pot was fresh fish from the lagoon and rice from the great fields of the Po valley.

Risotto con scampi

(rice and prawns) is one such classic, but the most famous Venetian rice dish is:

Risi e bisi

This is a spring dish of rice and new peas cooked with chopped onion, ham, and butter in a chicken stock, to create a soup that is eaten with a fork (an 'effete' implement introduced to disapproving Venetians by a Byzantine princess in 1005). Traditionally it was the first dish served at the Ducal Palace for the feast of St Mark on 25 April. It is now available all summer.

Fegato alla veneziana

The thinnest slices of calves' liver are fried with sliced onions for less than a minute, and rushed to the table. It is usually served with:

Polenta

A savoury dish made from yellow or white maize.

Carpaccio

This is a dish of paper-thin slices of fillet steak, garnished with fresh egg mayonnaise and finely slivered Parmesan. Some chefs have successfully replaced the mayonnaise with oil and lemon.

I dolci (sweets)

Venetians introduced cane sugar into Europe and the refining process was perfected here in 1471.

Aranci caramellizzati

Caramel oranges are a speciality of the Taverna Fenice.

Coffee

Coffee too was introduced into Europe via Venice, and the first coffee shop opened in the Piazza in 1683.

After reading the name of the wine on a bottle from the Veneto, one should look for the name of the producer. Although the province is divided into 3 DOC zones, *Denominazione di Origine Controllata*, these are only geographical descriptions, and no guide to quality. Most wine lists will have some of these names.

DOC Veneto

Soave
Italy's most famous crisp white wine is blended from 80 per cent Garanega grapes and 20 per cent Trebbiano. 10–11°
The Classico is grown in view of Soave's walls. 11½°

Bianco di Custoza
Made from a variety of grapes grown west of Verona.

Breganze Pinot Bianco
A blend of Pinot Bianco and Pinot Grigio. 11–12°

Bardolino
A splendid light red, blended from 4 grapes (Corvina, Molinara, Negara and Rondinella) grown on the shores of Lake Garda.

Valpolicella
The region's best-known red (the Corvina, Veronese, Rondinella and Molinara grapes).

Producers

Bertani	Bolla
Lenotti	Fratelli Tedeschi
Masi	Maculan
Pieropan	Tommasi

DOC Friuli-Venezia Giulia

Cabernet
A full red grown from the Cabernet Franc and Sauvignon. Best after 3 years. 13°

Tocai
A dry white, unconnected with the Hungarian Tokay.

Producers

Enofriulia	Bandut
Angoris	Livia Felluga
Bandut	Rubini
Valle	Jermann

DOC Trentino-Alto Adige

Chardonnay
Perhaps the best Chardonnay grown in Italy. 12°

Merlot
The Merlot grape makes a full red. 12–13°

Cabernet
This version ages well. 13°

Pinot Grigio
A good white, often *frizzante*.

Producers

Alois Lageder	Novalini
Bollini	Anton Lindner
Fratelli Pedrotti	Cavit
Laimburg	Lagarriavini

ARCHITETTURA

Venetians did not have to fortify their homes, but they did need them to be damp-proofed. The secret of standing a house in the lagoon was learned over 1,000 years ago, when oak piles, cut from the forests of Dalmatia, were hammered into the clay, where they slowly petrified in the salt water.

These were covered with horizontal planks of walnut or mahogany, and upon this platform, bricks were laid to bring the walls up to the waterline. The foundation was then sealed with 3 layers of waterproof Istrian stone.

The Facade

The early Venetian builders drew their inspiration from the east. The oldest surviving style is Byzantine, as at Ca' Farsetti (page 42). Even the later Gothic Ca' d'Oro shows eastern influence, and Ca' Dario,

illustrated here, although nominally a Renaissance design, is decorated with porphyry discs in the Byzantine manner. It took a foreigner, Jacopo Sansovino from Florence, to bring in the neo-Roman monumentalism, but it was just a facade. Behind it, the plan of the Venetian house remained much the same over five centuries.

Portego da Basso

The watergate opened on to an entrance hall that ran to a courtyard at the back. In former times this was the merchant's emporium, with storage rooms off either side.

Piano Nobile

The principal hall was on the 2nd floor, and also ran the full length of the house, with large windows at each end to provide light for the side rooms. The distinctive large-cowled chimneys were designed to trap sparks and help prevent city fires.

'When I search for a word to replace music,' said Nietzsche, 'I can only think of Venice.' 17th and 18thC visitors were overwhelmed by the music in the air. It is little wonder that the world's first public opera-house had opened here in 1637. The man who released the vocal solo into the theatre was Claudio Monteverdi. He is credited with having written the first real opera, *Orfeo*, which was performed in private at Mantua in 1607.

Despite his move to Venice as Maestro di Cappella at S. Marco, it was 22 years before Venetians heard the new art form, with a performance of his *Proserpina Rapita* at Ca' Dandolo (now the Danieli) in 1630. Seven years later, opera became a public entertainment when the Tron family opened the Teatro S. Cassiano (named after the parish church), and the Venetian appetite for the art became insatiable. For 200 years there were never less than seven companies, but they staged rather different kinds of productions to those seen today. There was little plot, as the singers, who commanded enormous fees, thought little of adding an aria that had nothing to do with the story, simply because it had won applause elsewhere. Alan Kendall tells how the castrato, Luigi Marchese, always entered from the top of a hill, regardless of the production, in a plumed helmet, armed with a sword and shield, to sing his own favourite aria before bothering to fulfil his obligation to the libretto.

Antonio Vivaldi, who was master of music at the Pietà, the conservatory for orphaned girls, alone wrote 44 scores. Yet he was equally famous as a violinist. What Monteverdi had done for the solo voice, Vivaldi was to do for the solo instrument. He wrote 450 concerti for string and wind instruments, some of which Johann Sebastian Bach admired enough to transcribe for the organ. His most enduring works are the four violin concerti, *The Four Seasons*.

Current programmes are published in *Un Ospite di Venezia*, from your hotel desk or tourist office.

CONSTITUTION

The Republic of Venice was the only government in the world to select its chief executive by lottery. Their reason was a fear of electing a tyrant. Originally the Doge had been elected by the entire population and, once elected, his power had been absolute. This had been much disliked, and in 1172 the Great Council had been formed, which, by 1229, obliged him to sign the *Promissione*. This was a list of all the things he could not do, and it was read to him once a year lest he forget it. Tyrants on the mainland, it was observed, were often military heroes swept into power on the popular vote. To safeguard Venetian democracy, the popular vote was abolished in 1297. (And military heroes were often thrown into prison to discourage ambition.) This created an oligarchy of ruling families, who voted in 1315 to close their Golden Book to any new members. To select the Doge, all the members of the Great Council over the age of 30 would receive, at random, a ballot ball. The holders of the 30 gold balls were reduced by a second lot to 9. These 9 then proposed 40 names which were voted upon, and so on. Once elected the Doge needed the advice and consent of various powerful committees; the most powerful of all, of which he was a member, was simply called The Ten. The Ten could order the death of anyone, including, as Doge Marin Falier discovered in 1355, the Doge. After the slight hiccup of his death, the system they called '*la Serenissima*' perpetuated itself serenely for 440 years.

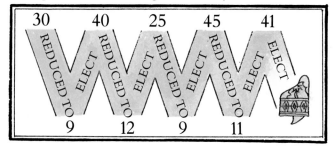

CARNIVAL

'**A**ll the world repairs to Venice to see the folly and madness of the Carnival,' reported John Evelyn in the 1640s. The word comes from the medieval Latin *carnem levare*, to leave meat. The celebration of farewell to meat began in Venice on St Stephen's day, 26 December. Any disguise, it was decreed, could be worn from that day until *Martedì Grasso* (Shrove, or fat, Tuesday).

However, the peculiarly Venetian disguise called a *baùtta*, comprising a black *tricorne* and cape, and a black or white mask known as the *larva* (ghost), could be worn by both men and women on feast days, and from 5 October to 16 December, but only in the afternoons.

The result was that the city appeared to be in a state of celebration for a full five months of the year, attracting an estimated 30,000 foreigners. It was very good business.

At the height of the festivities, bulls were loosed in the streets, and there was music, dancing and fireworks. It was also the season for opera and for gambling. Men dressed as women. Eggs filled with sweet water were thrown, and as Addison remarked in 1702, the disguises gave occasion to an abundance of love adventures. It all came to an end when the bells of S. Marco announced the time for the sprinkling of the ashes on Ash Wednesday. Like so many other Venetian institutions, Carnival was abolished by Napoleon. It was revived in the 1970s by the Mayor of Venice, although these days, the folly and madness only last two weeks.

La baùtta

La moretta

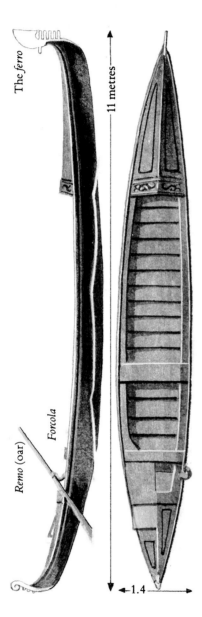

The ferro

11 metres

Forcola

Remo (oar)

←1.4→

The Gondola

The gondolier, in common with the psychoanalyst, has an hour of 50 minutes. Prices are set by the city, but should be agreed before embarcation. Originally gondolas were painted in many colours (they still are for Regata), but in 1562 they fell foul of the sumptuary laws against ostentation, and it was decreed that all 10,000 should be black. This edict seems to have coincided with a new mood of secrecy and the wearing of masks. In such a climate, the black gondola, with a black canopy, or *felze*, to hide passengers, was deliciously anonymous. Such craft, as depicted by Canaletto and Guardi, were comparatively crude alongside the modern gondola. Its sophisticated off-centre symmetry was finally perfected by the genius of Domenico Tramontin in the 1890s, just as the *vaporetti* were steaming in to deprive most gondoliers of their living.

Line ① Accelerato

The best way to see the canal is from one of the vaporetti, the 'little steamers' that no longer steam, since they've all been converted to diesel. Line 1 offers the most leisurely view, making every stop, all the way over to the Lido.

Line ② Diretto Motoscafo

The sleeker diretto makes fewer stops, giving the fastest ride between the station, the Rialto, and S. Marco. For the speed you pay slightly more, and it is likely to take a short cut through the less scenic Rio Nuovo.

Taxi

Always available, and always expensive. Telephone 5232326, or 5222303, or pick one up from the airport, S. Marco, the Rialto, the station, or the Lido.

Traghetto

A gondola ferry crosses the canal at 6 points marked on the maps. Passengers normally stand for the journey, which takes only a few minutes and costs but a few pence.

Ferrovia S. Lucia

Venice ceased to be an island city when the railway causeway was built in 1846. The station is dated 1955.

Vaporetto Stop

Line 1   Line 2 (Diretto)

Chiesa degli Scalzi

Its real name is S. Maria di Nazareth. The scalzi were the barefooted Carmelite Friars who founded the church in 1656. What they lacked in shoes, they made up for in a styles added. Today it is one of the 81 churches that have been either closed or demolished since the fall of the Republic, and is only open for concerts.

taste for the Baroque. They once had a marvellous Tiepolo ceiling, but it was despatched by an Austrian bomb in 1915. Two other Tiepolos remain, as do the ashes of Ludovico Manin, last of the Doges.

S. Simeone Piccolo
Little St Simon is perversely named, as it is clearly twice the size of the nearby S. Simeone Grande. It was completed in 1723, based in part on the Pantheon in Rome, but with many other

Ca' Foscari-Contarini
A Renaissance building.

Ponte degli Scalzi
Eugenio Miozzi designed this and the Accademia Bridge in the 1930s.

18 Canalazzo

This is what the Venetians call the Grand Canal. It follows the course of an ancient tidal flow, and is approximately 2¼ miles (3.5 km) long, and 15 feet (4.5 m) deep. The width varies from 130 to 230 feet (40–70 m). There is a speed limit of 9 km per hour (5½ mph) which is regularly broken by the emergency services.

Ca' Foscari
15thC Gothic.

Ca' Calbo-Crotta

Ca' is short for casa. During the period of the Republic there was only one palazzo in Venice, the Palazzo Ducale. Every other house, no matter how grand, was a casa. This collection of 15thC *houses is now the Hotel Principe.*

Rio Terrà

The name for a filled-in canal. Many were filled in during the 19thC.

Campo S. Simeone

Just as there was only one palazzo in Venice, there was only one piazza – the Piazza di S. Marco. Every other square was a simple campo – a field, and originally green.

20 Calle dello Spezier

The spezier *was an apothecary who dealt in spices, drugs and preserves. In the 17thC, two of his most prized 'medicines' were coffee and 'Indian salt' (sugar), but the pharmacists' monopoly on* these substances was lost after Venetians tasted the results of boiling them together in the Turkish manner, now called caffè antica.

known to have sired five illegitimate children, one by a nun called Celestina, but the official family planning led to the extinction of his and forty other families.

while sons were free to visit the thousands of courtesans for which Venice was famous. This accounts for the number of orphanages in the city and for the number of unmarried Doges. Doge Andrea Gritti is

Riva di Biasio

A butcher of this name is said to have murdered small boys to make his own original version of a pork delicacy called squazzeto alla boechera.

Ca' Gritti

Few Venetian nobles were permitted by their families to marry after the turn of the 16thC. To have done so would have put the family fortunes at risk. Daughters were despatched to nunneries,

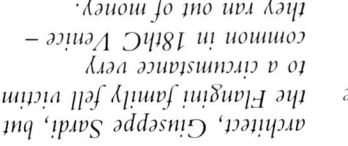

Scuola dei Morti

architect, Giuseppe Sardi, but the Flangini family fell victim to a circumstance very common in 18thC Venice – they ran out of money.

Ca' Flangini

There is a legend that it was inherited by two brothers, one of whom demolished his half of the building to spite the other. It is not true. The other half was never built. It was certainly planned by the

S. Geremia

The campanile is one of the oldest in the city, but the church was rebuilt in the 18thC. It now houses the remains of St Lucy of Syracuse, who was moved here in 1863 after her church was demolished to make way for the railway station. A painting of her by Palma Giovane, together with some relics, can be seen, on request, in the room to the right of the chapel.

Ca' Donà-Balbi

Ca' Marcello

Ca' Labia

The Labia family were fabulously wealthy. Gold plates were reputedly tossed out of the window to the gaudy pun 'L'abbia, o non l'abbia, saro sempre Labia' (Whether I have them, or not, I'll always be a Labia). To see the marvellous Tiepolo frescos of the life of Cleopatra, phone 781111 for an appointment. The building is now used by RAI, the broadcasting network.

Cannaregio

The Canale di Cannaregio, opposite, was, until the railway was built, the main entry to Venice from the mainland. The word means a marshy zone, and is the name of one of the six sestieri, administrative areas in the city.

24 **Ca' Querini-Papozze**

It was members of the Querini family who plotted the one insurrection against the constitutional government in 1310. To lead them they chose the popular Bajamonte Tiepolo but, forewarned, the Doge secretly prepared an ambush in the Piazza and the revolutionaries were routed. The insurrection ended when Tiepolo, mounted and ready to charge down the Merceria, had his standard-bearer killed

Palo

Like the gondola, its mooring pole is one of the symbols of Venice. Each is painted in the armorial colours of the house.

outright by a stone thrown by
an old lady from an upstairs
window.

Ca' Contarini
Built in the 17thC.

Ca' Gritti

Ca' Martinengo
Rebuilt in the 18thC.

Traghetto S. Marcuola
*This ferry service began in
1349.*

Ca' Giovanelli
15thC Gothic.

S. Marcuola

Dedicated to the two saints, Ermagora and Fortunato, this church has an interior by Giorgio Massari, and one of Tintoretto's paintings of the Last Supper. (Another is in S. Simeone Grande.)

Ca' Gatti

This has a splendid example of the Venetian altane (roof garden), where ladies used to sit wearing crownless hats, with their hair spread over large brims to bleach it a fashionable yellow.

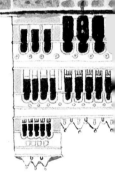

penultimate Byzantine Emperor, who spent three weeks here in 1438. In 1621 it was leased to the Turks as their fondaco and living quarters, which it remained until 1838. It was then

insensitively restored[7] and reopened as the city's Natural History Museum.
Hours: 9.00-13.30;
Sunday: 9.00-12.00.
Closed Monday.

Ca' Vendramin-Calergi

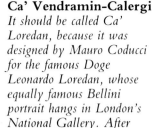

It should be called Ca' Loredan, because it was designed by Mauro Coducci for the famous Doge Leonardo Loredan, whose equally famous Bellini portrait hangs in London's National Gallery. After passing through the hands of two Dukes, it came to the Calergi family, who stipulated, when they sold it, that their name be retained. Today it houses the Casino in winter.

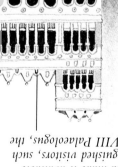

Fondaco dei Turchi
Built c. 1225, this Veneto-Byzantine house is one of the oldest in the city. The Dukes of Ferrara acquired it in 1381, and made it available for distinguished visitors, such as John VIII Palaeologus, the

Fondaco del Mégio
Fondaco comes from the Arabic fonduk, meaning warehouse. This was one built in the 15thC to store millet as a hedge against shortages. It has since been converted for use as a school.

Grimani Wing

In 1658, a nobleman was kidnapped, brought here and murdered on the instructions of the then owners, Pietro and Giovanni Grimani. An angry Republic razed the building to the ground and replaced it with a column of infamy. The wing was later rebuilt and, in 1882, hired by Wagner and his father-in-law, Franz Liszt. It was Wagner's last home. He died here of a stroke in 1883.

Ca' Belloni-Battagia

In 1647, with money to burn, Girolamo Belloni spent 150,000 ducats ($7½ million) buying himself into the nobility, and commissioning Baldassare Longhena to build this house. By the time it was finished, however, his luck had changed. Instead of moving in, he had to rent it out to Count Czernin, the imperial ambassador.

Ca' Marcello

The composer Benedetto Marcello was born here in 1686. Nineteen years later the city's theatres were outraged by an anonymous satire, Il Teatro alla Moda. *It was the work of Benedetto.*

Ca' Erizzo

15thC Gothic.

Ca' Emo

Ca' Soranzo

Ca' Priuli

Its Veneto-Byzantine origins can be seen on the ground floor.

Ca' Contarini-Duodo

15thC Gothic.

Ca' Tron

The Tron family only ever produced one Doge. They might have had a second in Filippo Tron, but that he was so fat that he actually burst, and died just a few days before the election in 1501.

Ca' Molin
A 17thC building.

┌ **Ca' Zulian**

Ca' Barbarigo
Tiepolo once painted a ceiling here depicting Strength and Wisdom, but it was removed to Ca' Rezzonico (page 53) where it can be seen in Room 7.

S. Stae
(St Eustace) The façade was the winning entry by Domenico Rossi in a competition of 1709.

Gallery of Oriental Art
Hours: 9.00–14.00;
Sunday: 9.00–13.00.
Closed Monday.

Hours: 10.00–16.00;
Sunday: 9.30–12.30.
Closed Monday.

Ca' Gussoni-Grimani

Tintoretto's frescos must still have been fresh on the facade when Sir Henry Wotton, England's first ambassador, took up residence for his second embassy in 1614. His name is in most dictionaries of quotations for his observation that 'An ambassador is an honest man sent to lie abroad for the good of his country.'

Ca' da Lezze

Gallery of Modern Art
Works by Rodin, Klimt, etc.

family home was begun by Longhena in 1652, but not completed until long after his death in 1710. Today it houses two art galleries:

Ca' Pesaro
It was the incompetence of Ambassador Francesco Pesaro, wrote Napoleon, that prompted him to declare the war that dissolved the Republic. What had been the

Ca' Fontana
Pope Clement XIII began life here as Carlo Rezzonico in 1693. He was the fifth Venetian Pope.

Ca' Giusti
Now an annexe to Ca' d'Oro.

Ca' d'Oro
This is the one Venetian house named, not after the owner, Marino Contarini, but after the gold leaf he lavished on the marble tracery on the facade, completed for him in 1440 by the brothers

remembered with pride by the city, so that when her home was replaced by this house by Domenico Rossi in 1724, it retained her name. Today it houses the Biennale Archives of Contemporary Art.

Ca' Corner della Regina
Caterina Corner became the most famous daughter of the Republic when she was crowned Queen of Cyprus in 1468. It was a brief, unhappy reign, but

Bon. Giorgio Franchetti, the last private owner, donated it and his collection of art to the state. The works include S. Sebastiano *by* Mantegna; *a* Venus *by* Titian; *and* paintings *by* Vivarini, Bellini, Guardi, Tintoretto, Carpaccio, Van Dyck, *etc.* Hours: 9.00–14.00; Sunday: 9.00–13.00. Closed Monday.

33

Ca' Favretto
In the 1870s Giacomo Favretto made this 14thC Gothic house his home and studio. Today it is the Hotel San Cassiano, but Favretto's paintings can be seen 4 doors down at Ca' Pesaro.

Ca' Morosini-Brandolin
15thC Gothic.

Ca' Foscari

Ca' Morosini-Sagredo
*The lower colonnade dates
from the 13thC.*

Ca' Pesaro-Rava
15thC Gothic

**Ca' Michiel dalle
Colonne**
*Eleven Byzantine columns
(more than on any other
building on the canal) give
the house its name.*

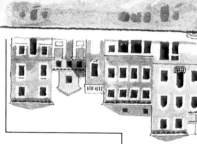

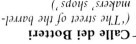

Calle dei Botteri
('The street of the barrel-
makers' shops')

Fondamenta dell'Olio
*Where olive oil was
unloaded.*

Pescaria
*Fishermen have sold their
catch here since the 9thC, but
they had to wait until 1907
to get this permanent roof
over their heads. On the side
is a statue of St Peter, the
fisher of men.*

Ca' Michiel dal Brusa
The Brusa was a fire which gutted its precedessor.

Ca' Mangilli-Valmarana
This was the home of Canaletto's English patron, Joseph Smith, called 'The Merchant of Venice' for the profits he was believed to have made at Canaletto's expense. He was also the patron of Antonio Visentini, who built this house for him in 1751.

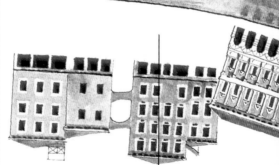

Erberia
Behind the fruit and vegetable markets are some curiously named streets. There are three named La Donzella (damsel), one Scimia (monkey), and one 'the street behind the Monkey'.

Traghetto S. Sofia
This ferry service started in 1363.

Calle delle Beccarie
('The street of the butchers' shops')

Ca' da Mosto

This 13thC Veneto-Byzantine house was the birthplace of Alvise da Mosto, the 15thC navigator. It later became the famous White Lion Hotel, where the Emperor Joseph II of Austria lodged 'incognito' in 1769. It was the worst-kept secret of the year.

Ca' Bolani-Erizzo

Pietro Aretino, Titian's notorious friend, lived in this

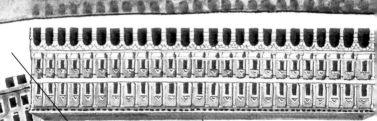

Erberia
Fruit and vegetable market.

Fabbriche Nuove
A 1555 design by Sansovino for the state offices of trade and commerce; now the Court of Assizes.

Fabbriche Vecchie
Built by Scarpagnino in 1522 to house offices of the court.

Ca' dei Dieci Savi
By Antonio Scarpagnino.

15thC house after being forced to flee Rome following the publication of his erotic sonnets. His acid, even blackmailing, pen earned him the title of 'Scourge of princes', but the Scourge was evicted for not paying his rent by Bishop Bolani, a prince of the church.

Ca' Civran
The offices of the Guardia di Finanza.

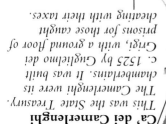

Ca' dei Camerlenghi
This was the State Treasury. The Camerlenghi were its chamberlains. It was built c. 1525 by Guglielmo dei Grigi, with a ground floor of prisons for those caught cheating with their taxes.

Fondaco dei Tedeschi

Built from public funds in 1508 to replace a building destroyed by fire, this was the warehouse, offices and hostel of the many German merchants in the city. It was originally decorated on the outside with frescos by Giorgione and Titian, frescos being cheaper than marble. Today it is the Central Post Office.

Sansovino and Palladio all submitted designs, but the public debt prevented any work for sixty years, by which time they were all dead. The present bridge opened in 1592, to the design of the appropriately named Antonio da Ponte. He built the arch high enough to allow a dismasted galley to pass underneath. The cost of the work was recouped by a toll.

S. Bartolomeo

Its proximity to the Fondaco dei Tedeschi made this the natural church of the German community, and Dürer, during his stay in 1506, painted his Madonna of the Rose Garlands to hang inside. Under Austrian rule it was removed to Prague, where it is now (damaged). The organ paintings of Sebastiano del Piombo remain, but you need to be up early to find the doors open.

Ponte di Rialto

The first bridge across the Rialto was destroyed in the Tiepolo uprising of 1310. The second collapsed under the weight of spectators viewing the wedding procession of the Marchioness of Ferrara in 1444. The third, a wooden drawbridge, is depicted in a painting by Carpaccio in room 20 of the Accademia. In 1524 a competition was called for a stone bridge. Michelangelo,

40 **Ca' Dolfin-Manin**

Built by Sansovino (c. 1560), this was the home of the last Doge, Ludovico Manin, who, in 1797, on the dissolution of the Republic, removed his ducal crown with the words, 'Take it, I shall not be needing it again.' Today the building houses the offices of the Banca d'Italia.

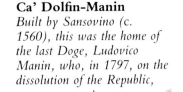

Fondamenta del Vin

In the absence of natural foundations, a fondamenta was built to support houses on the edge of water. This was also a street, and a quay where the city's wine ships unloaded.

Rialto

The name comes from Rivo Alto, or high bank; it was one of the first places in the lagoon to be settled. From its foundation, it was the city's financial and commercial centre.

Ca' Bembo
15thC Gothic, this was the birthplace of the scholar and poet Pietro Bembo, who in 1495 gave his name to the world's first classical typeface, Bembo, in which this book has been set.

Casetta Dandolo
This tiny 15thC Gothic house is said to stand on the birthplace of the blind Doge Enrico Dandolo, who masterminded and led the sack of Constantinople in 1204.

Ca' Valier
At the end of the street is the house where Giorgione died in 1510 (No. 1022, facing S. Silvestro).

Greek Consulate

Ca' Loredan

The King of Cyprus stayed here in 1362, and his royal coat of arms can still be seen on the upper loggia of this 13thC Veneto-Byzantine house, which now forms part of the Town Hall.

Ca' Farsetti

In the absence of a Doge, it is the Mayor who rules Venice, presiding over a Giunta chosen from an elected council here at the Town Hall, formerly a 13thC merchant's house.

Traghetto S. Silvestro

Crosses over to the Calle and Fondamenta del Carbon, where coal was once unloaded.

Ca' Rava

Despite the Gothic appearance, this house was built in 1906, on the supposed site of the palace of the Patriarchs of Grado.

Ca' Corner–Martinengo

James Fenimore Cooper stayed here, and so did Turner, who sketched from the top floor when it was the Hotel Leone Bianco.

Ca' Corner–Valmarana

Ca' Grimani

Although Sanmicheli built this as a private home for Girolamo Grimani and his family in 1556, its forbidding facade seems better suited to the present occupants, the Courts of Appeal.

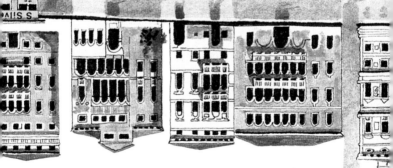

Veneto-Byzantine.
Ca' Businello

12thC Veneto-Byzantine.
Ca' Barzizza

44

Ca' Corner-Contarini
Built c. 1450, it's nicknamed 'dei Cavalli' because of the horses in the two coats of arms.

Ca' and Casetta Tron
15thC Gothic.

Ca' Martinengo
In the 16thC this house was frescoed by Pordenone. It was later owned by Count Volpi, who founded the CIGA hotel chain, brought electricity to Venice and launched the Venice Film Festival. He

Ca' Papadopoli
Giangiacomo Grigi of Bergamo built this for the Coccina family around 1560. The adjacent garden was created by the Papadopoli in the 19thC.

Ca' Donà
Another Veneto-Byzantine house. It was much altered in the 16th and 17th centuries.

also devised the industrialization of Mestre and Porto Marghere, in the hope of bringing wealth back to the city.

Ca' Benzon
In 1818, this was the rendezvous of the smart set; Byron, Canova and others flocked to the presence of the Contessa Marina Benzon who inspired the love song 'La Biondina in Gondoletta'.

Ca' Donà della Madonnetta
It is named after a small 15thC relief of the Madonna on the facade, but the house is a much older Veneto-Byzantine design.

Ca' Bernardo
Perhaps the architect was drunk when he drew the plans for the first and second piani nobili (main floors) of this 15thC Gothic house, for they are completely out of alignment.

46

Ca' Curti
A 17thC building.

Ca' Corner-Spinelli
The first house in Venice to employ Renaissance elements in its design, it was built by Mauro Coducci for the Lando family between 1490 and 1510. It was then sold to the Cornaro family who engaged Giorgio Vasari, the Florentine, to paint nine ceiling panels, which have since been dispersed.

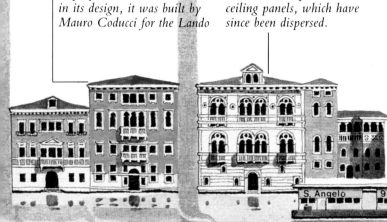

Ca' Grimani
One of Venice's first Renaissance houses (1520). and formed a collection of paintings that now hangs in London's National Gallery.

Ca' Cappello-Layard
Sir Austen Layard, the discoverer of the ruins of ancient Nineveh, lived here

Ca' Barbarigo
Called 'della Terrazza' because of the terrace.

Teatro S. Angelo

One of Venice's seven opera-houses once stood here. They were all named after parish churches. Some twenty of Vivaldi's forty operas were produced here, beginning with Orlando Finto Pazzo in 1714, and ending with Feraspe in 1739.

Ca' Garzoni

15thC Gothic, it is now part of the University of Venice.

Ca' Pisani-Moretta

After Chiara Pisani inherited this 15thC Gothic house in 1737, she embarked on a programme of embellishment that was to last thirty years. To help fund the work, she spent twenty-five of those years trying to disinherit her brother on the grounds that he was illegitimate. She failed. Her descendants have recently restored the house, which still has a fine Tiepolo ceiling.

Traghetto Garzoni

Crosses to S. Tomà (Frari).

Ca' Mocenigo-Nero

This 16thC house was unlucky for Giordano Bruno, invited here in 1592 to reveal the secrets of alchemy. His host was dissatisfied, and denounced him to the Holy Office, who removed him to Rome, where he was burnt at the stake. His ghost is said to have returned to haunt the house of his betrayer.

Traghetto S. Tomà

This ferry began operating in 1354. There were once 13 such crossing points on the canal, now reduced to 6. Traghetto comes from the Latin, transgerere, to go beyond.

Ca' Tiepoletto

15thC Gothic, with later additions.

Ca' Giustinian-Persico

A 16thC house.

Ca' Mocenigo

Byron stayed here in 1818, and wrote the beginning of Don Juan, inspired, no doubt, by his own adventures, one of which ended with the lady flinging herself into the canal from this balcony.

Ca' Mocenigo Vecchia

The Countess of Arundel entertained Antonio Foscarini here in 1621. His enemies accused him of selling secrets, and he was executed, but the Republic apologized on discovering his innocence.

Ca' Civran-Grimani
A 17thC building.

Ca' Dolfin

Ca' Dandolo-Paolucci
This is now the Danish Consulate.

Ca' Marcello dei Leoni

Ca' Contarini delle Figure

The 'figures' are under the balcony and difficult to see. It was built in 1546 for Jacopo Contarini, the botanist and senator, whose job it was

Ca' Masieri

Frank Lloyd Wright was not permitted to build here.

was feted here in 1574. Today, it's the university's Institute of Economics.

Ca' Balbi

Nicolo Balbi camped out in a boat awaiting the completion of this house, but died of a cold before it was finished in 1590. Alessandro Vittoria designed it. Napoleon used it to view the Regata of 1807. Today it seats the regional government.

to devise the dazzling spectacles that so bemused Henry III of France when he stayed in Ca' Foscari (opposite) in 1574.

Ca' Erizzo
15thC Gothic.

Ca' Foscari
This was the starting and finishing point of the Regata. It was also the first 4-floor house in the city, built for Doge Francesco Foscari in 1437. Henry III of France

Ca' Giustinian
In 1172 a naval disaster reduced the Giustinian family to a single monk. On petition, the Pope temporarily released him from his vows to marry the Doge's daughter. They produced a family of twelve, some of whose descendants built these houses in 1452. Wagner stayed in the second to write Tristan in 1858.

Ca' Moro-Lin

A member of the Moro family did jealously murder his wife Disdemona, providing Shakespeare with the plot of Othello. He wasn't black however, and the family were not Moors, but came from Morea, in Venetian Greece. In 1670, the painter Pietro Liberi joined two Gothic buildings to create this 'House of the Thirteen Windows' that we see today.

Carlo Rezzonico left here to become the Republic's fifth and last Pope, Clement XIII. Robert Browning made his last visit here in 1889, caught a cold and died. Today it is the museum of 18thC Venetian furnishings and paintings. (By Guardi, Longhi, Tiepolo, etc.) Hours: 10.00–16.00; Sunday: 9.00–12.00. Closed Friday.

Ca' Grassi
This was the last great house to be built on the canal, designed in the 1730s by Giorgio Massari. It has recently been bought and restored by FIAT, who have reopened it for exhibitions.

S. Samuele
Dedicated to the prophet Samuel, this rarely used church has frescos of the Paduan school and a 12thC campanile.

Traghetto S. Samuele

S. Samuele 2

Ca' Rezzonico 11

Ca' Rezzonico
Baldassare Longhena began this house for the Bon family in 1667, but they had to sell it in 1712, half finished, to the Rezzonico family for whom Massari completed it in 1750. Eight years later,

Ca' Contarini-Michiel – *Built in the 17thC.*

Traghetto S. Samuele

Ca' di Madame Stern – *A 19thC building.*

54 Ca' del Duca

Francesco Sforza, Duke of Milan, planned the largest house in Venice when he acquired this site in 1461. But the project never got beyond the rusticated foundations on the right-hand side. Resentful of his policies, the Republic seized his property, later selling it to become the two houses that we see today. Titian had a studio in one of them throughout 1514.

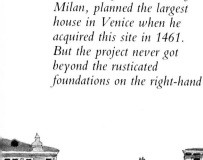

Ca' Loredan

When in 1752 the Austrians were seeking a site for their embassy, they were offered this 15thC Gothic house on terms that were both simple and extortionate: 29 years' rent in advance, plus all maintenance costs. Being both diplomats and realists, they accepted. The owner, Francesco Loredan, had just been elected doge.

Ca' Moro

Ca' Falier
During the American civil war, William Dean Howells, the author of Venetian Life, *stayed here as the United States consul. The two roofed terraces are rare survivals of what Venetians called a* liago.

Ca' Giustinian-Lolin
An early design of Longhena, it now houses the Fondazione Levi centre of music.

Ca' Contarini degli Scrigni
Built as an extension to its Gothic neighbour in 1609, this house takes its name from the scrigni, or money-chests that came into the family as part of a 15thC dowry.

Ca' Contarini-Corfù
15thC Gothic.

Ca' Gambara

turning the former S. Maria della Carità (with Monastery and Scuola) into the Accademia. It houses the greatest treasury of Venetian paintings in existence. Entry is made through the former Scuola, the facade of which was designed by Giorgio Massari. Guide on page 114.
Hours: 9.00–14.00;
Thursday: 9.00–16.00;
Sunday: 9.00–13.00.
Closed Monday.

Ca' Querini
Now the British Consulate.

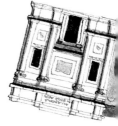

Ca' Marcello
Now the Consulate of West Germany.

Ponte dell'Accademia
Built in 1932 by Eugenio Miozzi to replace a 19thC Austrian iron bridge.

Ca' Franchetti

Baron Franchetti, who gave Ca' d'Oro and its treasures to the city, has been much criticized for his 'arbitrary restoration' of this 15thC house, and particularly for the wing he added in 1896.

Accademia delle Belle Arti
Napoleon demolished thirty churches in Venice, but this one he merely secularized,

Ca' Contarini-Polignac
Its Renaissance façade belies a Gothic interior.

Ca' Brandolin-Rota
Now part of the Accademia.

A parade of the famous passed through this house after the Curtis family of Boston acquired it in the 19thC. Monet and Sargent each had a studio here; Browning gave recitations;

Henry James stayed to write The Aspern Papers *and used the house as a setting for* The Wings of the Dove. *Cole Porter 'Opened in Venice' with a brief stay in 1923, before moving on to*

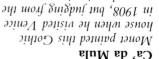

Ca' da Mula
Monet painted this Gothic house when he visited Venice in 1908, but judging from the canvas hanging in Washington's National Gallery, it was only the watergate that took his eye.

Ca' Barbarigo
In the 19thC there was an unfortunate mode for mosaics. These were by Carlini.

Ca' Loredan

Ca' Balbi-Valier

open what Diaghilev called
'an idiotic nightclub on a boat
moored outside the Salute'.
The house is really two
buildings, the second added in
1694 to accommodate a
ballroom – a pressing need.

Canova, the last great
Venetian sculptor, had his
studio here in the 1770s.
Later, during the First World
War, the poet Gabriele
d'Annunzio spent his last
days in blindness here.

Ca' Biondetti

Rosalba Carriera, the
pastellist, died here in 1757.
Her portraits had an
international reputation, and
her visit to Paris in 1721 had
a strong influence on the
growth of the French Rococo
movement. A small room of
her work can be seen at Ca'
Rezzonico, and a few more,
including a self-portrait, hang
in Room XVII of the
Accademia.

The builder and architect, Sansovino, often had to stop work on this house while the Corner family quarrelled over whose share of the family inheritance should be used to pay him, with the result that he died in 1570 before it was finished. Following the fall of the Republic, it was occupied by the Austrian Governor. Today it houses the Prefecture of Police.

spoiling their view of the lagoon (which it would have, judging from the architect's model that survives in the Correr Museum). Peggy Guggenheim bought it in 1951 to house her collection of modern art. Included are works by Klee, Picasso, Braque, Chagall, Ernst, etc.

Hours: 12.00–18.00; Saturday, 12.00–21.00. Closed Tuesday, and from November through March.

Ca' Minotto

Girolamo Minotto was the last bailo (head of the trade mission) in Constantinople before it fell to the Turks in 1453. He dispatched urgent warnings to Venice, but help arrived too late.

Ca' Barbarigo
A 17thC building.

Ca' Venier-Contarini
Also from the 17thC.

Traghetto S. Maria del Giglio

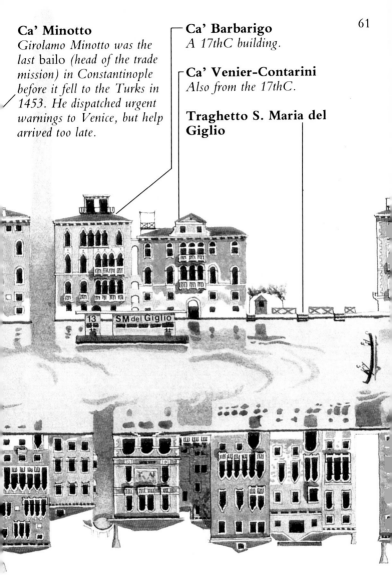

Ca' Venier dei Leoni

It was called 'Ca' Nonfinito' when work stopped with only the ground floor finished in 1749. Some say the Veniers ran out of money; others that the owners of Ca' Grande, opposite, objected to it

Ca' Dario

It's just a façade, but the prettiest on the canal, added in 1488 to the Gothic house of ducal secretary Giovanni Dario. Its originality suggests that Dario may have designed it himself.

Ca' Pisani-Gritti

The Giorgione frescos had long faded from the outside of this 15thC house when Ruskin stayed here in 1849. That was before it became the famous Gritti Palace Hotel of today.

Ca' Manolesso-Ferro

15thC Gothic, it now houses offices of the regional administration.

Ca' Flangini-Fini

Attributed to the architect Alessandro Tremignon.

Ca' Salviati

Ca' Genovese
Built in 1892.

canal on a bridge made of boats.

to prevent the structure sinking, despite the support of over a million oak piles. The main doors open once a year, on the feast of the Salvation (21 November), when a votive procession crosses the

Ca' Contarini-Fasan

This is popularly known as the house of Desdemona, although the luckless lady was murdered by her jealous husband well before it was built in the 15thC. Only one room wide, it gained its name from a member of the Contarini family who liked shooting pheasant.

Ca' Contarini
Also 15thC Gothic.

Salute

14

S. Gregorio
An ex-abbey.

S. Maria della Salute
The great plague of 1630 claimed 50,000 lives. Those who survived built this church in thanks for their deliverance. Their architect, Baldassare Longhena, had to build a wooden dome

Calle di Traghetto
A reminder of a discontinued ferry service.

Ca' Tiepolo
At the turn of the 19thC this was the Hotel Britannia. It is now the Europa & Regina.

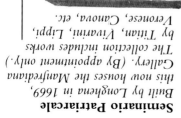

Dogana di Mare
The ever-changing weather-vane of Fortune tops the gilded globe of the Customs House. The Lady has been turning to catch the wind in her little bit of metal drapery since 1676.

Seminario Patriarcale
Built by Longhena in 1669, this now houses the Manfrediana Gallery. (By appointment only.) The collection includes works by Titian, Vivarini, Lippi, Veronese, Canova, etc.

Ca' Treves

Built in the 17thC, it still houses the two Canova statues of Ajax and Hector – in a special hall on the mezzanine floor of the adjacent building – that were viewed by Metternich and the Emperor Joseph II of Austria. It is not open to the public.

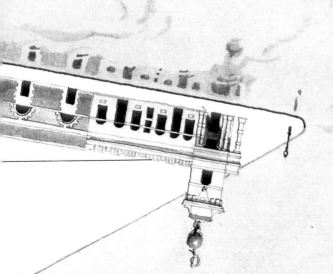

Hotel Bauer Grünwald

This 19thC Gothic facade is far more pleasing than its modern counterpart at the other end, facing S. Moisè.

Ca' Giustinian

In the 19thC it was the Europa Hotel, where Verdi stayed while producing his operas at La Fenice. Other guests included the poet Théophile Gautier and Marcel Proust. Today it is the headquarters of the Venice Biennale, the international exhibition of modern art held every even year. There are permanent pavilions in the Giardini Pubblici (see rear endpaper) and other exhibits elsewhere in the city.

Il Ridotto

In 1768, Marco Dandolo opened the Ridotto (reduced quarter, or foyer) of his house as a gambling casino. It was soon one of the most famous in Europe. To enter you had to be either a noble, or masked. Six years later the nobles closed it. They were losing too much money to those wearing masks. Today it is a theatre.

Hotel Monaco

Harry's Bar

This is the original, named after Harry Pickering, an American who borrowed some money from a bartender, and was so grateful that he later returned to help launch the bartender, Giuseppe Cipriani, in this business. Giuseppe's fruit juice and champagne cocktails are named after Venetian painters; a Bellini, with peach juice, and a Tiziano, with grapefruit juice and grenadine. His most famous dish, thin slices of raw beef with mayonnaise, is named after Carpaccio.
Today the business is run by his son Arrigo (Harry), who claims to be the only man named after a bar.

Zecca

This was the mint, where the Republic's gold ducats, known as zecchini, or sequins, were minted. Built by Sansovino in 1547, it was paid for by the sale of liberty to 25,000 Turkish slaves in Venetian Cyprus.

Libreria Marciana

This is Sansovino's masterpiece, but he was thrown into jail in 1545 after the ceiling collapsed. They had to let him out to repair it, but at his own expense. Palladio thought it the most beautiful building since antiquity.

Giardinetti Reale

The gardens were created when the old Republican granaries were swept away.

Old Library

Only seen by special permission of the Director.

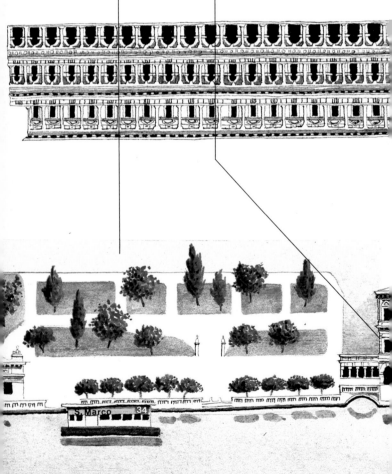

Archaeological Museum

Founded in 1523, there are now twenty rooms of Greek and Roman antiquities.

Twin Columns

As a reward for raising these two columns, Niccolò Starantonio, nicknamed the swindler, was granted his request to run a gambling den at their feet. By chance, it was also decreed that it should be a place of execution and that the bodies of criminals strangled elsewhere should be hung from the columns by their feet. The columns are crowned by the lion of St Mark and St Theodore with his alligator-dragon.

PIAZZA
DI SAN MARCO

Napoleon called it the finest drawing-room in Europe and then promptly demolished one end, destroying Sansovino's church of S. Giminiano to make way for his 'Royal Palace', now called the Ala Napoleonica, the entry for

Procuratie Vecchie

These were the offices and residence of the State Procurators, the administrators.

The Correr Museum

The city museum of art and Venetian history. The art gallery, with works by Gentile Bellini and Carpaccio, is on the second floor; the historical collections of documents, robes, and coins etc. are on the first.
Hours: 10.00–16.00
Sunday: 10.00–12.30
Closed Tuesday.

Procuratie Nuove

Built by Sansovino when he altered the shape of the piazza, changing it from a rectangle to a trapezium (wider at one end).

Florian's

Europe's first coffee-house started near here in 1683.

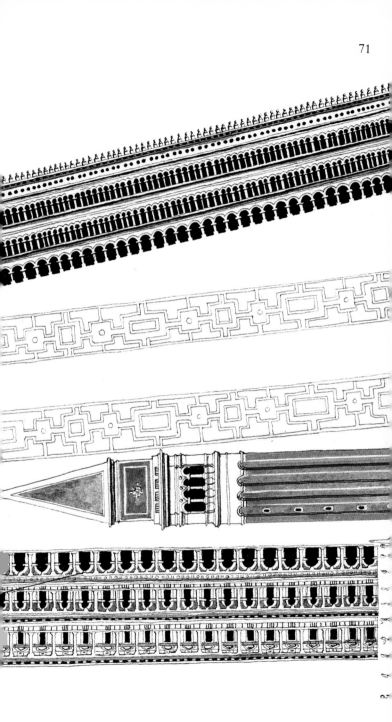

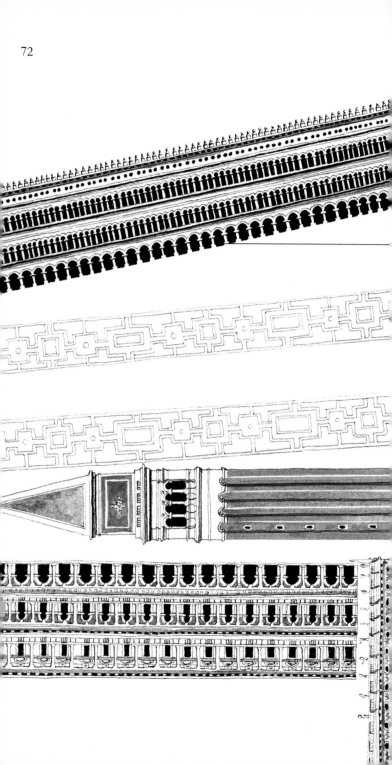

Torre dell'Orologio
Built in 1499 by Mauro Coducci. A staircase can be climbed to the top, to see the 'Moors' strike the hour. At Epiphany, and during the week of Ascension, they are joined by the figures of a herald angel and the Magi.

Quadri
The great rival café to Florian's, it has a rival orchestra that fills the air with rival compositions.

Campanile
It was begun in 888, but six centuries elapsed before it was completed in 1514. Its sudden collapse into a heap of dust in 1902 was far more rapid, yet not a soul was hurt. It was rebuilt exactly as it had been. An elevator will lift you to the top for a marvellous view, but beware: above your head swings the great bell, the Marangona, to mark the hour.

Pavement
The large white squares marked the sites of market stalls for the various craftsmen's guilds. It was completed in 1735.

BASILICA DI

Of all the objects stolen to embellish this jackdaw's nest of a cathedral, none was more spectacular than the first, the body of St Mark the evangelist. Taken from his tomb in Alexandria, he was smuggled past Muslim customs officials in a basket marked pork, and spirited to Venice and a hero's welcome in 828. To legitimize the theft, a prophecy was produced that claimed the Apostle had actually visited the lagoon in his lifetime. Swept in, it was said, by a tempest, and deposited on the Rialto, where he fell asleep and dreamed of being spoken to by an angel, who said, '*Pax tibi Marce Evangelista. Hic requiescet corpus tuum.*' ('Peace, Mark. Here your body will rest.') To validate the tale, these words were to be repeatedly engraved in stone for the next thousand years. The first church was consecrated in 832, only to be burned down in the uprising of 976. It was replaced by the sumptuous brick building that stands behind the stone cladding we see today. The oldest in the city, it was consecrated in 1094, as the Doge's private chapel, but effectively it was the state church where all Doges were crowned and many buried. It didn't become a cathedral until Napoleon decreed it, after the fall of the Republic, in 1807.

The Four Bronze Horses
The only *quadriga* to survive from classical times, they were removed from the Hippodrome in Constan-

tinople by the Venetians in
1204. Napoleon carried
them off to Paris in 1797,
but they were returned at
the end of his regime in
1815. What you see are
copies. The originals shelter
from pollution in the

Museo Marciano

This occupies 4 rooms
behind the horses.

Gothic Sculpture

Best seen from the gallery,
the work was begun in 1358,
and completed in the 15thC.

Gilded Towers

Each contains a statue of an
Evangelist.

Mosaics

The finest, and only original, work is over the door
on the left depicting the
translation of the body of St
Mark to the Basilica as it was
in the 13thC.

SECOND DOOR:
The magistrates adoring the
body (Sebastiano Ricci,
1718).

CENTRAL DOOR:
The Last Judgement (1836).

FOURTH DOOR:
Venice welcoming the body
of St Mark.

FIFTH DOOR:
The removal of the body
from Alexandria.

Upper Mosaics

Descent from the Cross
Descent into Hell
The Resurrection
The Ascension

Bas-reliefs

Hercules carrying the Ery-
manthian boar (Roman)
St Demetrius (Byzantine)
Hercules and the Hydra
St George
The Madonna
Archangel Gabriel

Central Arches

Beautiful carvings dating
from c. 1235–65.

BASILICA DI

Zen Chapel

This was the great ceremonial entrance from the lagoon, until Cardinal Zen decided that he would like a memorial chapel dedicated to himself inside the Basilica. There was no room, but Zen was the nephew of the Venetian Pope Paul II and, even more important, he had left a large bequest to the Republic on condition that his wish be granted. Being, as always, short of funds, the Republic unceremoniously closed the ceremonial door lest the bequest disappear.

Pietra del Bando

Decrees of the Republic were proclaimed from this stump of porphyry brought back from Acre.

Porta dei Fiori

The 'Door of Flowers' has a 13thC Nativity, surrounded by angels, flowers and prophets.

Sarcophagus

Of Daniele Manin who led the uprising against the Austrians in 1848. The short-lived republic was crushed the following year.

Byzantine Madonna

Black candles used to be lit on either side to comfort those about to be executed in the Piazzetta.

The Tetrarchs

Venetians like to believe that these were 4 foreigners turned to stone for trying to steal from the treasury. In fact, the Venetians stole them from Constantinople. They represent the Emperor Diocletian and his three co-rulers, and were carved in Egypt in the 4thC.

Pilastri Acritani

These two trophies may have been carried off from Acre in 1256. They are thought to have been carved in Syria in the 6thC.

The Virtues

They were carved in the 15thC by Piero di Niccolò Lamberti.

Bas-relief

Alexander the Great being carried to heaven in a chariot drawn by 2 griffins.

Pope John XXIII

Inside the doorway is a bust of the former Patriarch of Venice, the popular Angelo Roncalli.

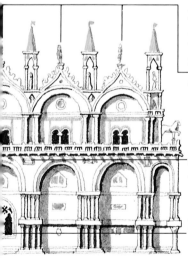

BASILICA DI

Pala d'Oro

The earliest part of the gold altar screen was ordered from Constantinople in 978. The last artist, Boninsegna, left his signature on it in 1342. It is encrusted with 1300 pearls, 300 sapphires, 15 rubies, 90 amethysts, 400 garnets, 75 balas-rubies, 4 topazes and 2 cameos. Below the central figure of Christ Pantocrator stand the Virgin and the Empress Irene.

Chapel of the Madonna of Nicopeia

Byzantine emperors used to carry this icon into battle (Nicopeia means 'maker of victory') but in 1204 the Madonna granted the Venetians the victory, allowing them to sack Byzantium and bring her here. Thieves prised out her jewels in 1979, but their victory was short-lived.

Chapel of St Isidore

The saint's remains were brought from the isle of Chios in 1125. His story is told in the mosaics.

Chapel of the Madonna dei Mascoli

is named after members of a 17thC male confraternity.

Romanesque Stoup

Altar of St Paul
Altar of St James
Chapel of the Crucifix

The crucifix is another trophy from Constantinople.

Iconostasis

8 marble pillars divide the nave from the sanctuary, and support the statues of the Virgin, St Mark and the 12 Apostles (*c.* 1394).

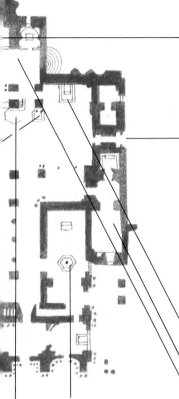

Sarcophagus of St Mark
(beneath the high altar)
Many think that the body of
the saint perished in the fire
of 976. It was certainly miss-
ing in 1094, when Doge
Vitale Falier instituted a
search for it. Falier was
rewarded on 25 June that
year by a miracle. Amidst
prayers for the revelation of
the hiding place, there came
a shaking and a falling of
stones, and the arm of the
saint suddenly appeared
from behind a pier near the
altar of the sacrament.
(Recorded in a mosaic
nearby.) The event is
piously described as the
Inventio, or 'the Invention'.

Ducal Entrance
This is normally closed.

Altar of the Sacrament

The Treasury
With the exception of the
'Seat of Mark' (*c.* 630) and
the ducal throne (*c.* 1500),
most of the treasures are
Byzantine, from the sack of
Constantinople; some of the
best works were later
plundered by Napoleon in
the sack of Venice in 1791,
and his treasury melted
them down.

Baptistery
The font was designed by
Sansovino, *c.* 1545. Opposite the entrance is the
sarcophagus of Andrea
Dandolo, the last Doge to be
buried in S. Marco.

Pulpit
This was where the Doge
was shown to the people
after his coronation.

Chapel of S. Clemente
The entry to the sanctuary.

MOSAICS OF

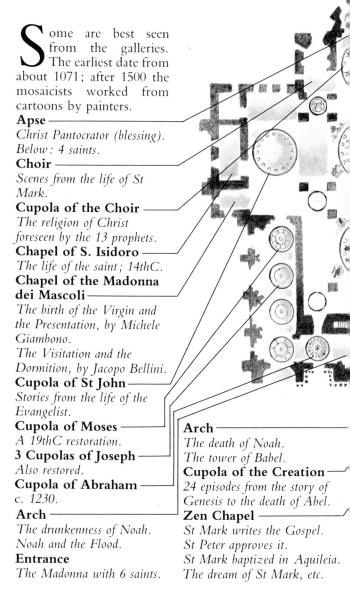

S ome are best seen from the galleries. The earliest date from about 1071; after 1500 the mosaicists worked from cartoons by painters.

Apse ————————
Christ Pantocrator (blessing). Below: 4 saints.

Choir ————————
Scenes from the life of St Mark.

Cupola of the Choir ————
The religion of Christ foreseen by the 13 prophets.

Chapel of S. Isidoro ————
The life of the saint; 14thC.

Chapel of the Madonna dei Mascoli ————————
The birth of the Virgin and the Presentation, by Michele Giambono.
The Visitation and the Dormition, by Jacopo Bellini.

Cupola of St John ————
Stories from the life of the Evangelist.

Cupola of Moses ————
A 19thC restoration.

3 Cupolas of Joseph ————
Also restored.

Cupola of Abraham ————
c. 1230.

Arch ————————
The drunkenness of Noah. Noah and the Flood.

Entrance
The Madonna with 6 saints.

Arch ————————
The death of Noah.
The tower of Babel.

Cupola of the Creation ——
24 episodes from the story of Genesis to the death of Abel.

Zen Chapel ————————
St Mark writes the Gospel.
St Peter approves it.
St Mark baptized in Aquileia.
The dream of St Mark, etc.

Choir
*The transport of the body of
St Mark from Alexandria.*

Sacrament
*The rediscovery of St Mark.
The miracle of Christ.*

Cupola of the Ascension
*Christ ascends. Below stand
the Virgin, 2 angels and the
12 apostles. Between the
windows are the 16 virtues.*

Cupola of St Leonard
*The 4 saints Nicholas,
Blaise, Clement and Leonard.*

Vault
*The Entry into Jerusalem.
The Temptation of Christ.
The Last Supper.
The Washing of the Feet.*

Corners
*The 4 Evangelists and the 4
rivers.*

The Passion
*The kiss of Judas.
The Crucifixion.
The 3 Marys at the Tomb.
Incredulity of St Thomas.*

Cupola of the Pentecost
*The winged Holy Ghost
enlightens the 12 Apostles,
who teach the nations between
the 16 windows.*

Right Aisle
*The Madonna with prophets.
Christ in the Garden.
The Acts of the Apostles.*

Corners
4 large angels.

The Baptistery
*Font cupola: the 12 Apostles
immerse 12 converts, while
below 4 doctors of the Greek
church comment.
Altar cupola: Christ and the
9 heavenly choirs.
The life of St John the
Baptist.
The banquet of Herod with
the dance of Salome.*

PALAZZO

This was the official residence of the 120 Doges who ruled Venice between 809 and 1797. It took its present shape when the lagoon facade was completed in 1404, and that on the Piazzetta 20 years later. A disastrous fire in 1577 meant that it had to be rebuilt. Palladio designed a classical building, but the Council wisely decided to keep their Gothic classic.

Porta della Carta
The Paper Gate, where decrees were once affixed, is the entrance; it was carved by the Bon family. Above the door kneels Doge Francesco Foscari.

Judgement of Solomon
On the corner, carved by Pietro Lamberti.

Fatal Pillars
The ninth and tenth pillars are slightly darker than the rest. Executed criminals were often hung between them as a warning.

Central Balcony
Doge Andrea Gritti prays before the Lion of St Mark.

Archangel Michael
Adam and Eve
Central Balcony
The Dalle Masegne carved the statue of Justice.

Giants' Staircase
Named after Sansovino's statues of Mars and Neptune, symbolizing Venetian power on land and sea.

Courtyard Facade
Redesigned by Antonio Rizzi after a fire in 1483.

Scala d'Oro
It was only used by nobles and honoured guests.

Bridge of Sighs
Named after the despair of those about to be either incarcerated or executed.

New Prison
Casanova escaped, but not from this building. He had been held for two years in the *piombi*, the wooden cells in the palace under the roof, over which he climbed to his freedom in 1756. It was Venice's first jail break, for which the jailor was sentenced to ten years in his own dungeons.

Ponte della Paglia
Barges loaded with straw (*paglia*) used to moor here.

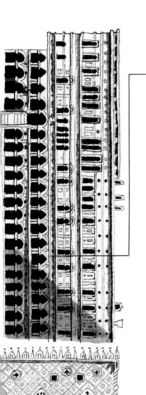

Scala d'Oro
*Designed by Sansovino;
gilded stuccoes by Vittoria.*

SECOND FLOOR

DUCAL APARTMENTS

ROOM 1

Sala degli Scarlatti
*This was where dignitaries
donned their scarlet robes.
The ceiling is by Biagio and
Pietro da Faenza; the
fireplace is by the Lombardi.*

ROOM 2

Sala dello Scudo
*The reigning Doge's armorial
shield (scudo) was always
kept here, the main waiting-
room to his private quarters.
The maps were drawn in
1540 and updated in 1762.*

ROOM 3

Sala Grimani
*Doge Grimani's arms are in
the centre of the ceiling. The
painted frieze is by Vicentino
and the chimney by the
Lombardi.*

ROOM 4

Sala Erizzo
*Another Lombardi fireplace
and a frieze, Putti and the
Trophies of War, by
Lorenzetti.*

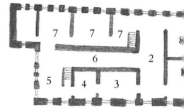

ROOM 5

Sala degli Stucchi
*Framed in the stuccoes are
works by*
Tintoretto
Henry III of France
Bassano
Adoration of the Shepherds

ROOM 6

Sala dei Filosofi

DUCALE

The 12 statues of
philosophers have vanished.
Titian
St Christopher (1524)

ROOM 7

Museum of Painting
Carpaccio
The Lion of St Mark
Hieronymus Bosch
Various works

ROOM 8

Room of the Squires
G. B. Tiepolo
Venice and Neptune

THIRD FLOOR

ROOM 9

Atrio Quadrato
*The ceiling of the Square
Hall was painted by
Tintoretto
Doge Girolamo Priuli
Receives the Sword of Justice*

ROOM 10

Sala delle Quattro Porte
*Designed by Palladio, the
Room of the 4 Doors was the
waiting-room to the Senate.*
Titian
*Doge Antonio Grimani before
the Faith*
Tintoretto
*Ceiling of Jove Entrusting
Dominion over the Adriatic
to Venice.*

ROOM 11

Anticollegio
*This was where the
illustrious waited for an
audience in the Collegio.*
Veronese
The Rape of Europa
Tintoretto
*The Wedding of Ariadne
Minerva Dismisses Mars*

PALAZZO

Vulcan's Forge
Mercury and the 3 Graces
Jacopo Bassano
Jacob's Return to Canaan
The ceiling is by Marco del
Moro, the fireplace by
Scamozzi.

ROOM 12

Collegio
Here the Doge assembled
with the Six Savi, the leaders
of the Council of Ten, and
the Chancellor (always a
citizen, not a noble).
A Campagna fireplace.
Veronese
Doge Sebastiano Venier
Gives Thanks for the Victory
of Lepanto
Tintoretto
Marriage of St Catherine
Doge Nicolò da Ponte at
Prayer to the Virgin
Doge Alvise Mocenigo Gives
Thanks at the End of the
Plague

ROOM 13

Sala del Senato
The Senate ceiling is the
work of Cristoforo Sorte with
the centre painted by
Tintoretto
The Triumph of Venice
BEHIND THE THRONE:
Descent from the Cross, with
Doges Lando and Trevisan

LEFT WALL:
Palma Giovane
Venice and Doge Venier
Receiving the Homage of
Subject Cities
Doge Cicogna at Prayer
Allegory of the League of
Cambrai
END WALL:
Doges Lorenzo and Girolamo
Priuli at Prayer
Tintoretto
Doge Loredan at Prayer

ROOM 14

La Chiesta
The Doge's private chapel.
Sansovino
Carved Madonna and Child.

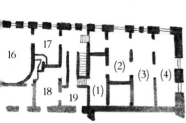

Aliense
Adoration of the Magi
Marco Vecellio
*Pope Clement VII and the
Emperor Charles V*

ROOM 17

Sala della' Bussola
*This room has a 'Lion's
Mouth' for the deposit of
secret denunciations.*
WALLS:
Marco Vecellio
*Doge Donato at Prayer to the
Virgin*
Aliense
*The Conquest of Bergamo
The Conquest of Brescia*

ROOM 18

Sala dei Tre Capi
*The three leaders of the
Council of Ten had unlimited
power to investigate crimes of
sedition or espionage and their
decision was final. The
fireplace is by Jacopo
Sansovino and the ceiling by*
Gianbattista Zelotti
The Victory of Virtue

ROOM 19

Saletta dei Inquisitori
Tintoretto
*Return of the Prodigal Son
(a copy)*

ROOM 15

Antichiesta

ROOM 16

Consiglio dei Dieci
*The Council of Ten (actually
there were 17) met to try
political crimes. The term of
office was 12 months.*
Veronese
*Old man in Eastern Costume
Jove Strikes down the Vices
(a copy; the original was
taken to the Louvre)*
WALLS:
Leandro Bassano
*The meeting of Doge Ziani
and Pope Alexander III*

Armoury, see page 90.

SECOND FLOOR

ROOM 20

**Andito del
Maggior Consiglio**
This has a ceiling by
Domenico Tintoretto.

ROOM 21

**Sala della Quarantia
Civil Vecchia**
The old civil courtroom.
Andrea Celeste
Moses

ROOM 22

Sala del Guariento
*This has the remains of
Guariento's huge painting
from the old Great Council.*

ROOM 23

**Sala del
Maggiore Consiglio**
*The immense hall was large
enough to take all 1,700
members of the Venetian
aristocracy who formed the
Great Council. The 1577 fire
destroyed the original
paintings and frescos, which
had to be replaced.*
Tintoretto
*Paradise (The largest oil
painting in the world.)*
CEILING:
Veronese

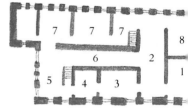

The Apotheosis of Venice
LEFT WALL *(facing throne)*:
The Life of Barbarossa, by
The Caliari
The Bassani
Tintoretto
Andrea Vicentino
Palma Giovane
Paolo dei Franceschi
Federico Zuccari
Girolamo Gambarato
Giulio del Moro
RIGHT WALL:
The Fourth Crusade, by

ROOM 25

Sala dello Scrutinio
This was the counting-room, where the votes cast by the Great Council were assessed.
ABOVE THE THRONE:
Palma Giovane
The Last Judgement
RIGHT WALL:
Andrea Vicentino
The Defence against Pepin
Sante Peranda
The Battle of Jaffa
Aliense
The Conquest of Tyre
Marco Vecellio
Defeat of Roger II of Sicily
LEFT WALL:
Tintoretto
The Venetians at Zara
Andrea Vicentino
The Capture of Cattaro
The Battle of Lepanto
Pietro Liberi
Victory at the Dardanelles
The Triumphal Arch was built in honour of Francesco Morosini in 1694.
A frieze of the 120 Doges continues into this room from the Great Council.

ROOM 26

Private Apartments
G. B. Tiepolo
Venice and the Homage of Neptune

Jean Leclerc
Andrea Vicentino
Tintoretto
Aliense
Palma Giovane
Carlo Saraceni
END WALL:
Veronese
Triumph of Doge Contarini.

ROOM 24

Sala della Quarantia Civil Nuova
The new civil court.

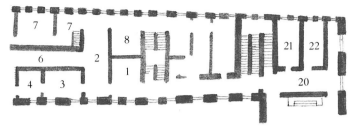

THIRD FLOOR

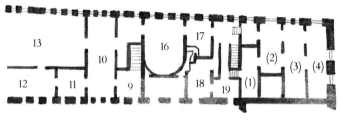

SECOND FLOOR

ROOM 27

Statues of Adam and Eve by Antonio Rizzo.

ROOM 28

Giovanni Bellini
Pietà
The Armoury
In these rooms are collected the ceremonial arms of the Council of Ten, together with captured trophies and gifts to the Republic. In all, approximately 2000 items are on display.

ROOM 1

The equestrian armour of Erasmo Gattamelata.

ROOM 2

The Venetian-made armour of King Henry IV of France and a Turkish standard from the battle of Lepanto.

ROOM 3

The Morosini Room

ROOM 4

A room of firing pieces.

ATLAS

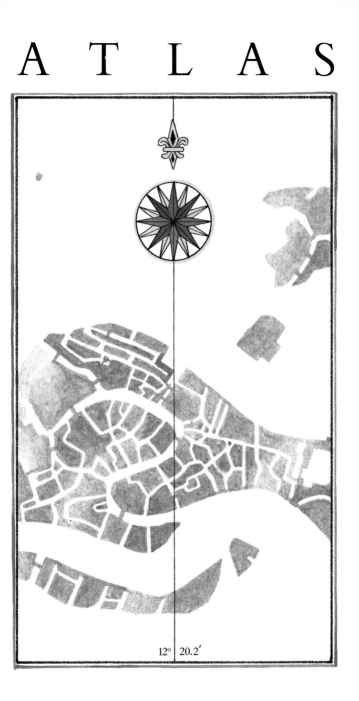

12° 20.2′

92 Ferrovia S. Lucia

Poor St Lucy was martyred in Syracuse in 304. Her remains were moved to Constantinople, where the Venetians found her in 1204, and removed her to this site. Palladio built her a church, but it was knocked down in 1863 to make way for the railway station, and she was moved, once more, to nearby S. Geremia (page 22) from which she was recently stolen by gangsters, but recovered. This is the second station to bear her name, built in 1955.

Giardino Papadopoli

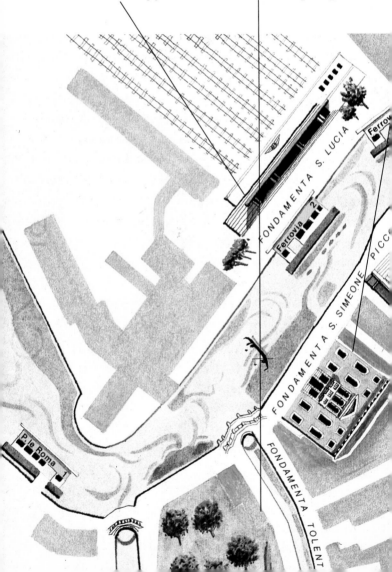

Ca' Diedo

Ca' Cappello

S. Simeone Piccolo
Described in the Canal section, page 17.

S. Simeone Grande
Also called S. Simeone Profeta, this small church is decorated with Tintoretto's Last Supper, with an altarpiece by Palma Giovane, The Presentation in the Temple. The earliest work is an effigy of S. Simeone by Marco Romano (c. 1318).

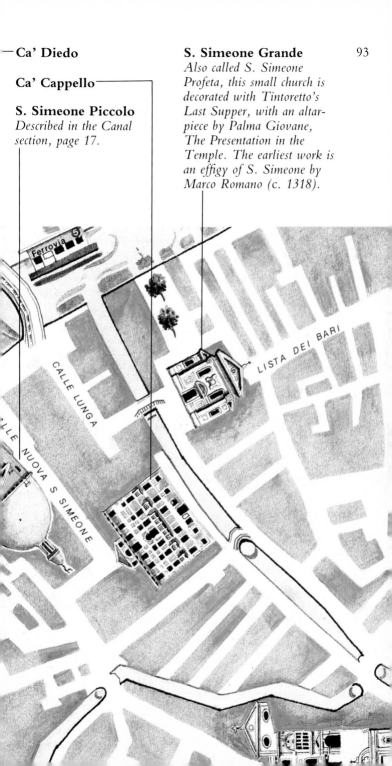

S. Giacomo dell'Orio

Founded in the 9thC, this jackdaw's nest of a church has a fine ship's-keel ceiling, marble columns looted from Byzantium and a collection of paintings by Veronese, Lotto and Palma Giovane. Open 7.30–12.00 and 17.00–20.30.

Traghetto S. Marcuola——

S. Zan Degola

In Venetian, this means John the Beheaded. The Baptist's church is now deconsecrated and used for concerts. Some of the 11thC murals have gone to S. Giacomo dell'Orio, others to be restored.

Riva di Biasio

RIVA DI BIASIO

LISTA DEI BARI

RUGA BELLA

Campo
S. Giaco
dell'Or

Verre da Pozzo

Surrounded by water they could not drink, Venetians trapped rainwater in these wells, of which some 600 were built. The water entered at the sides and was filtered through layers of gravel and sand. A public official came to unlock the iron lids twice a day. The only alternative supply was imported at considerable expense from the river Brenta.

Ca' Sanudo

The home of the 16thC diarist Marin Sanudo.

S. Stae

SALIZZADA S. STAE

CALLE TINTOR

Ca' Pesaro
Opening hours: page 30.

S. Maria Mater Domini
Often closed, this Renaissance church contains a 12thC Byzantine relief of the Madonna, and a painting of St Christina by Vincenzo Catena (c. 1520).

Ponte delle Tette
According to the diarist Marin Sanudo, there were a staggering 11,654 registered courtesans in the city at the beginning of the 16thC. But they had competition from transvestites from the mainland. To encourage heterosexuality, the ladies were

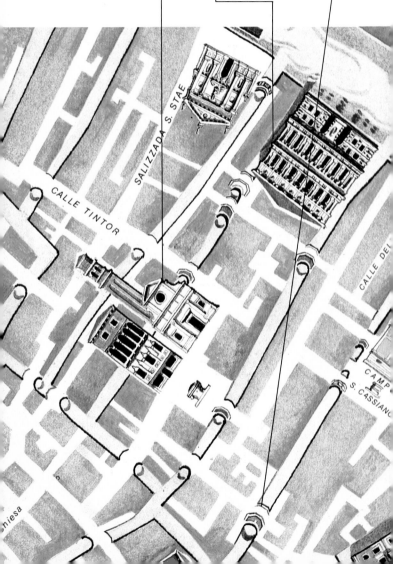

permitted, by law, to solicit with bared breasts on what became known as the Ponte and Fondamenta delle Tette.

S. Cassiano

Behind the harsh exterior hangs Tintoretto's painting of the Crucifixion.

Banco Giro

Private banks were abolished in 1587 after 96 of them had defaulted. It was then found that a state bank was a good way to fund the public debt. With guaranteed interest, depositors could giro (turn) bonds over to third parties at a profit.

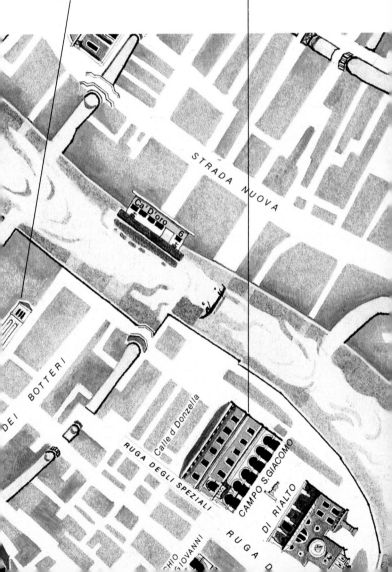

Scuola Grande di S. Rocco

In 1564, Venice's artists were invited to submit drawings for the decoration of the Scuola. In secret, Tintoretto painted an entire ceiling panel, smuggled it into position, and unveiled it (to the chagrin of his competitors) to win the commission that lasted 23 years. His cycle of 50 canvases has made the building his monument. Hours: 9.00–13.00; 15.30–18.30.

Frari

Floor-plan on next page.

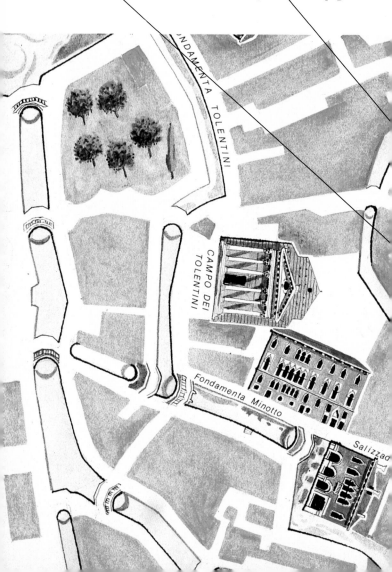

S. Rocco

The remains of the French saint St Roch were stolen from Montpellier in the belief that they would protect Venice from the plague. His first church opened in 1489, but was rebuilt, several plagues later, in 1725 (the facade in 1771). Tintoretto painted four canvases of the saint for the interior.

Archivio di Stato

1,000 years of history gather dust on 36 miles of shelving in this 300-room former Franciscan monastery.

Calle dell' Olio

CAMP
S. STI

RIO TERRA S. TOMA

CAMPO
S. ROCCO

CAM

I FRARI

S. Maria Gloriosa dei Frari was finally completed after 100 years of work in October 1338. It was then decided to pull it down and put up something even bigger. This is it, consecrated in 1492.

Chapel of St Mark
with a 1474 triptych by Bartolomeo Vivarini *of the saint.*

Milanese Chapel
The altarpiece was begun by Alvise Vivarini *but on his death it was completed by Marco Basaiti.*

Franciscan Chapel
The altarpiece is by Bernardino Licinio *The Madonna and Franciscans also: 5 Martyrs.*

Chapel of St Peter
The altarpiece was carved by the Dalle Masegne school.

Pesaro Monument
Jacopo Pesaro had it carved in his lifetime by the Lombardo brothers so that he could appreciate their work.

Titian
The Ca' Pesaro
Madonna
Painted between 1519 and 1526, it was commissioned by Bishop Jacopo Pesaro, who kneels on the right.

Monument to Doge Pesaro
Designed by Longhena.

Canova Monument
When Canova designed this monument to Titian in 1794, there was no money and the Republic was about to collapse. On his death in 1827, the design was realized with the help of many

Giovanni Bellini
*Masterpiece of the Virgin
Enthroned with Saints.*
Frangipane
Pietà
Titian
The Assumption
*In 1518, it was a
revolutionary work. Titian
had brought the theatre into
the church and the Friars at
first refused to accept it.*
Altar of the Relics
by Cabianca (1711).
Tomb of Doge Dandolo
*with a lunette above by
Paolo Veneziano
Madonna and Child and
Saints*
Bernardo Chapel
*The polyptych is by
Bartolomeo Vivarini
Virgin and Child and Saints.*
**Chapel of
the Sacrament**
Chapel of St John
*with a wooden statue by
Donatello
of St John the Baptist.*
**Monument
to Doge Foscari**
by Antonio Bregno (1457).
**Monument
to Doge Tron**
by Antonio Rizzo (1476).
The Choir
*The wood engravings are by
the Cozzi family (c. 1468).*

*donations from all over
Europe.*
Altar of St Catherine
Palma Giovane
St Catherine of Alexandria.
Alessandro Vittoria
Sculpture of St Jerome.
Altar of St Anthony
with a painting by F. Rosa.
Titian's Monument
A mid-19thC creation.

S. Giovanni Evangelista
15thC but rebuilt in the following two centuries.

Scuola S. Giovanni
Now an art gallery and exhibition centre, it has a fine barrel-vaulted double staircase by Mauro Coducci (1498) up to the Salon.

Ca' Centani-Goldoni
Carlo Goldoni was born here in 1701 to become Venice's most famous playwright. He wrote his 136 comedies in what is now a Museum of Theatre. (Entry at the top of the stairs; admission free.) Hours: 8.30–13.30. Closed Sunday.

Calle dell' Olio

CAMPO S. STIN

Calle d

RIO TERRA S. TOMA

CAMPO S. ROCCO

CAMPO S. TOMA

CALLE D

Ca' Michiel-Olivo
15thC Gothic.

S. Polo
Under the 13thC ship's-keel ceiling are paintings by Tintoretto, Veronese, and the remarkable 14 Stations of the Cross by G. D. Tiepolo. The campanile is c. 1362.

Ca' Corner-Mocenigo
There is a better facade on the Rio S. Polo.

Ca' Soranzo
Casanova entered this 14thC house as a hired fiddler for a ball. He left it ennobled, as the adopted son of a sick senator he had helped.

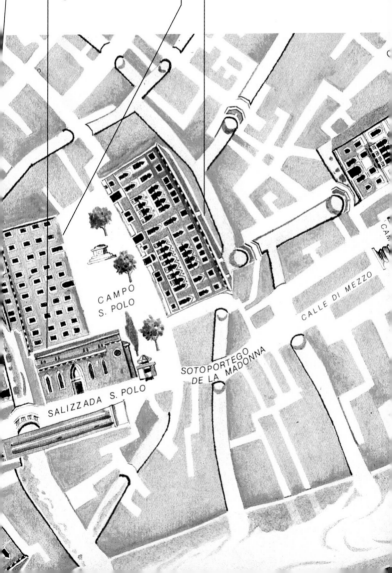

CAMPO
S. POLO

CALLE DI MEZZO

SOTOPORTEGO
DE LA MADONNA

SALIZZADA S. POLO

104 Ca' Cappello

When the noble Bianca Cappello ran off with a Florentine bank clerk in 1563, the city was outraged, and the two were sentenced to death in absentia. In Florence, she discovered her husband's poverty, while Francesco de' Medici discovered her beauty. She became first his mistress and later, after the unhappy demise of her husband in a dark alley, his Grand Duchess. At this, Venice commuted the death sentence, and hailed her 'Daughter of the Republic'.

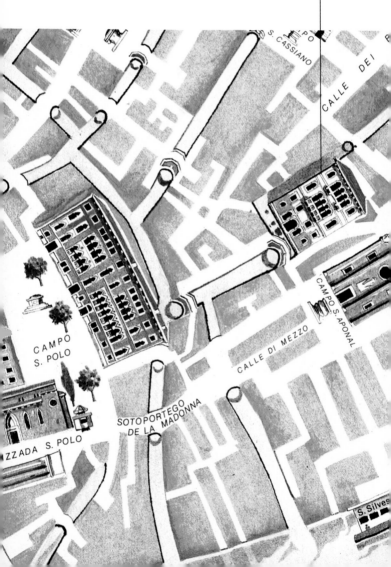

S. CASSIANO

CALLE DEI

CALLE DEI

CAMPO S. APONAL

CAMPO S. POLO

CALLE DI MEZZO

SOTOPORTEGO DE LA MADONNA

ZZADA S. POLO

S. Silves

S. Aponal
Closed, but you can see some late 13thC carvings over the doorway.

S. Silvestro
It contains Tintoretto's Baptism of Christ, and Girolamo da Santacroce's picture of St Thomas à Becket.

S. Giovanni Elemosinario
Inside is Titian's painting of St John the Almsgiver.

S. Giacometto
Founded in 421, this is the oldest church in Venice; the present building dates from the 11thC.

Scuola dei Carmini

The upper hall has a fine
ceiling painted by G. B.
Tiepolo depicting St Simon
Stock's vision of receiving the
scapular of the Carmelite
order from the blessed Virgin.
This was two pieces of cloth
joined by string, believed to
relieve the pain of purgatory
immediately after death.
Hours: 9.00–12.00;
15.00–18.00.

Ca' Rezzonico ────────
Opening hours on page 52.

Scuola dei Varotari
(tanners), now an art school.

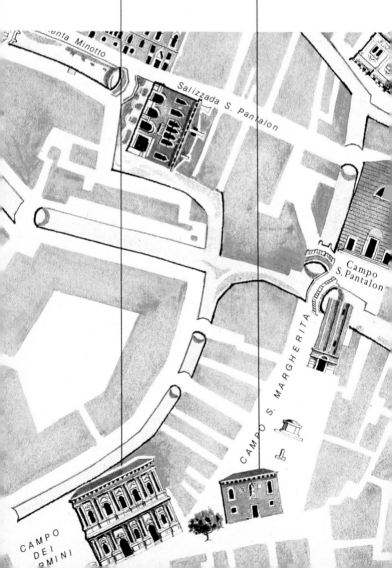

S. Pantalon
Inside is a giant ceiling painting of the martyrdom and apotheosis of S. Pantalon. It was the last work of Gian Antonio Fumiani, who had barely laid the last brush stroke when he slipped off the scaffolding and plunged to his death. Another last work is that of Veronese (second chapel on the right).

S. Tomà
Closed for restoration.

Vigili del Fuoco
The boats of the fire service have no shortage of water.

Carmine

In the 14thC S. Maria del Carmelo you'll find Cima da Conegliano's painting of the Adoration of the Shepherds (over the second altar on the right). Opposite is one of the rare Lotto pictures remaining in Venice: St Nicholas with John the Baptist, St Lucy,

etc. Giuseppe Sardi's 16thC campanile was struck by lightning in 1776 while the monks were ringing the bells. One died in his haste to desert the good work.

Ognissanti

Closed. It is now a hospital.

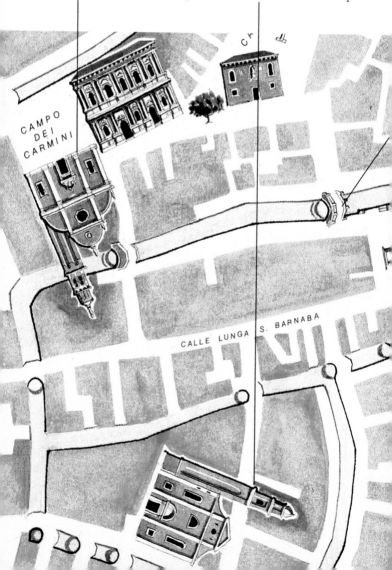

Ponte dei Pugni

The Bridge of Fists was one of several places where pitched battles took place between the Castellani and the Nicolotti. The four white footmarks show where the combatants stood, but without the modern parapets they were soon in the canal.

S. Barnabà

In the last days of the Republic this was the parish church of many impoverished nobles who had been granted free apartments in the area. Finished in 1776, it has a ceiling fresco by Costantino Cedini. The campanile dates from the 14thC.

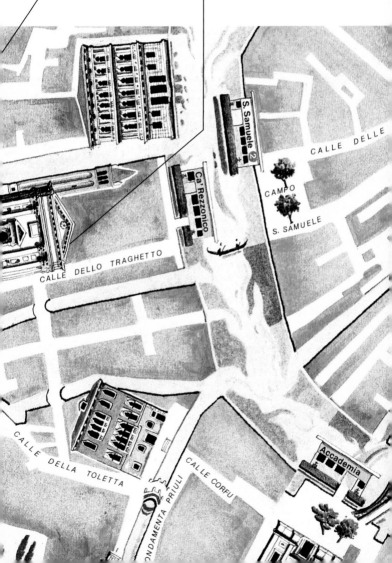

S. Trovaso

Trovaso is a corruption of Gervasio and Protasio, two saints whose church, with its two entrances, provided common ground to the rival factions, the Nicolotti and the Castellani. In the event of a wedding between them, the Castellani used the south *door, the Nicolotti the one on the Rio. Paintings by Palma Giovane and Tintoretto, and Giambono's equestrian St Chrysogonus.*

Squero S. Trovaso
One of the last 3 gondola yards (squeri) in the city.

Ca' Nani
15thC Gothic.

S. Maria della Visitazione
With a fine coffered ceiling.

I Gesuati
The order of the Poveri Gesuati was suppressed in *1668. The Dominicans, who took over, commissioned Giorgio Massari to build this church, and G. B. Tiepolo to fresco the ceiling and to paint the canvas on the first altar on the right.*

S. Agnese

Scuola S. Spirito
Now a private house.

S. Spirito
Built in 1483, this church is open only on Sunday.

St George
Anglican services are held each Sunday.

Traghetto di S. Giglio

Ca' Cenedese
If the door of No. 175b is open, feel free to enter and watch the glass-blowers at work. There is no charge, and there is no need to buy.

CAMPO
S. VIO

CALLE D CHIESA

FOND. ZORZI

175

FONDAMENTA SORANZO D FORNACE

FONDAMENTA CA' BALA

RIO TERRA S. VIO

ZATT

FONDAMENTA

Abbazia S. Gregorio

This was one of the oldest monasteries in the city until closed by the Napoleonic regime. Today the church is used as a centre for the restoration of pictures.

Catecumeni
Closed.

S. Maria della Salute

To commemorate the plague that killed his colleague, Giorgione, Titian painted the Sacristy altarpiece of St Mark with four saints. On the ceiling are three later works, and opposite the entrance hangs Tintoretto's Marriage at Cana.

Salute 14

ECUMENI

ACCADEMIA

ROOM 1

Venetian Gothic Paintings
Alvise Vivarini
Holy Father
Domenico Campagnola
4 Prophets
Jacobello del Fiore
Justice and Archangels
Coronation of the Virgin
Madonna of the Misericordia
Paolo Veneziano
*Coronation of the Virgin and
stories from the life of Christ
and St Francis*
Madonna Enthroned
Lorenzo Veneziano
Sts Peter and Mark
Annunciation and 4 Saints
Marriage of St Catherine
Polyptych: Annunciation
Jacobello Alberegno
Triptych: Crucifixion
Stefano Veneziano
Polyptych of the Apocalypse
Jacobello del Fiore
Coronation of the Virgin
Madonna of the Misericordia
Michele Giambono
Coronation of the Virgin
St James and Saints
Venetian School
Triptych of the Madonna
Nicolò di Pietro
Madonna and Child (1394)
Antonio Vivarini
Madonna and Child
Michele di Matteo
Polyptych: S. Helena

Venetian School
Madonna
Jacopo Moranzone
Polyptych: The Assunta

ROOM II

Carpaccio
*10,000 Martyrs of Mount
Ararat*
*Presentation of Christ in the
Temple*

ACCADEMIA

ROOM III

Benedetto Diana
Madonna and Child
Cima da Conegliano
Madonna and Saints
Deposition
Giovanni Buonconsiglio
3 Saints
Bartolomeo Montagna
Madonna and St Sebastian
and St Jerome
Follower of Giorgione
Sacred Conversation

ROOM IV

Jacopo Bellini
Madonna and Child
Giovanni Bellini
Madonna and Child between
St Paul and St George
Madonna and Child and Sts
Mary Magdalene and Catherine
Madonna and Child Blessing
Hans Memling
Portrait of a Young Man
Cosmè Tura
Madonna and Child
Piero della Francesca
St Jerome in the Desert
Andrea Mantegna
St George

ROOM V

Giovanni Bellini
Head of the Redeemer
Madonna of the Trees
Pietà
Madonna and Child

Marco Basaiti
Prayer in the Garden
Calling the Sons of Zebedee
Giovanni Bellini
Sacra Conversazione
Pietà
Cima da Conegliano
Madonna of the Orange Tree
Incredulity of St Thomas
Madonna Enthroned with
Saints

Giovanni Bellini
Madonna and Child with the Baptist and Saint
Madonna dei Cherubini Rossi
Giorgione
Old Woman
The Tempest
Giorgione revolutionized Venetian painting. In technical terms he abandoned the old hard edge in favour of a soft outline, but more importantly he is credited with having invented the easel painting, the portable work that could be hung in a private room. His choice of subjects was equally revolutionary. The glory of God, or of the state, was abandoned for caprice, for his own pleasure. These are the only two works that survive in Venice. The meaning of the old woman clutching the piece of paper with the words Col tempo *(with time) is clear, but the significance of* The Tempest *is as much a mystery today as it was in the 16thC. Vasari complained of not having understood any of Giorgione's frescos of the Fondaco dei Tedeschi and, he added, he had not met anyone who had. We cannot judge, as they have long since disappeared.*

ROOM VI

Paris Bordone
Presentation of St Mark's Ring
Bernardino Licinio
Portrait of a Lady
Tintoretto
Madonna dei Camerlenghi
Titian
St John the Baptist

ACCADEMIA

Giovanni Cariani
Portrait

ROOM VIII

Palma Vecchio
Sacra Conversazione
Andrea Previtali
Crucifixion
Christ Child in the Manger
Gerolamo Romanino
Entombment
Rocco Marconi
Christ and the Adulteress
Pordenone
Madonna Enthroned
Bonifazio
Paintings removed from the Ca' dei Camerlenghi.
Venetian School
Visitation

ROOM IX

Sante Zago
Tobias and the Archangel
Titian
Symbols of the Evangelists
Bonifazio
God the Father and the Piazza

ROOM X

Tintoretto
St Mark Freeing the Slave
Miracle of St Mark
Dream of St Mark
Transport of the Body of St Mark
Crucifixion

Bonifazio
Lazarus the Beggar
Palma Vecchio
St Peter and Saints

ROOM VII

Lorenzo Lotto
Gentleman in his Study
Bernardino Licinio
Portrait of a Lady

ACCADEMIA

Paolo Veronese

In 1573, Paolo Veronese was commissioned to paint the Last Supper for the monks of SS. Zanipolo, but they were unhappy with the result and the Inquisition were called in to question Veronese. 'Why,' they asked, 'are there dogs and dwarfs in your painting?' 'And what,' they inquired with menace, 'was meant by the presence of Germans?' (a code word for Protestants). Veronese could only plead artistic licence, which was rejected, and he was ordered to alter the picture at his own expense. Which he did. He changed the name to Christ in the House of Levi.

Titian

Pietà
Procurator Jacopo Soranzo

ROOM XI

Jacopo Bassano
St Jerome

Paolo Veronese
Allegory of Venice (ceiling)
Madonna Enthroned
Annunciation
Marriage of St Catherine

Luca Giordano
Deposition
Crucifixion of St Peter

Tintoretto
Adam and Eve

Cain and Abel
The Creation of the Animals

Bernardo Strozzi
Feast in the House of Simon

G. B. Tiepolo
St Helena discovers the True Cross
Frieze of the Miracle of the Bronze Serpent

ACCADEMIA

Procurator Cappello
Jacopo Bassano
Andrea Schiavone
Palma Giovane

ROOM XIV

Jan Lys
Sacrifice of Isaac
Tiberio Tinelli
Luigi Molin
Bernardo Strozzi
Doge Francesco Erizzo
Domenico Fetti
David
Meditation
The Good Samaritan

ROOM XV

Giandomenico Tiepolo
Abraham and the Angels

ROOM XVI

G. B. Tiepolo
Rape of Europa

ROOM XVIA

G. B. Piazzetta
Fortune-teller
Domenico Pellegrini
Bartolozzi, the Engraver
Alessandro Longhi
Tommaso Temanza
Allegory
Giuseppe Nogari
Head of an Old Woman
Vittore Ghislandi
(also called **Fra Galgario***)*
Count Vailetti

ROOM XII

Francesco Zuccarelli
Giuseppe Zais
Marco Ricci
*Landscapes, bacchanals and
hunting scenes*

ROOM XIII

Tintoretto
Doge Alvise Mocenigo

ACCADEMIA

ROOM XVII

Canaletto
Capriccio of a Colonnade
This is the only painting by
Andrea Canal, called
Canaletto, to remain in
Venice. He donated it to the
Accademia on his election in
1763.
Bernardo Bellotto
The Scuola di S. Marco
Francesco Guardi
Isola di S. Giorgio
Fire at S. Marcuola
Pietro Longhi
6 scenes from Venetian Life
Rosalba Carriera
7 pastels, including a
self-portrait
G. B. Tiepolo
Transfer of the Holy House
from Nazareth to Loreto (a
sketch for the destroyed ceiling
of the Scalzi)

ROOM XVIII

Canova
Statuettes

ROOM XIX

Boccaccio Boccaccino
Marriage of St Catherine
Marco Basaiti
St James
St Antony
Portrait
Dead Christ
St Jerome

Marco Marziale
Supper at Emmaus
Carpaccio
Sts Anne and Joachim
Bartolomeo Montagna
St Peter and Donor
Antonello de Saliba
Christ at the Column
Agostino da Lodi
The Washing of the Feet

ACCADEMIA

Carpaccio
The Miracle of the Cross at the Rialto
Giovanni Mansueti
Healing of a Sick Child
The Brothers Fail to Take the Relic inside S. Lio for the Funeral of One who has Disparaged it
Gentile Bellini
Recovery of the Relic from the Canal of S. Lorenzo
The Healing of Pietro de' Ludovici
The Procession in the Piazza di S. Marco
Benedetto Diana
A Child falling from a Ladder is Saved
Lazzaro Bastiani
Filippo de' Masseri Offers the Relic to the Scuola di S. Giovanni

ROOM XXI

Carpaccio
The Legend of St Ursula
1. St Ursula and her 11,000 Virgins
2. The English Ambassadors Demand Her Hand for Hereus Son of King Conon
3. Ursula Delays the Marriage for a Pilgrimage to Rome; the Conversion of Hereus
4. The Departure of the Ambassadors to England and King Conon Reads the Terms

ROOM XX

In 1396, Filippo de' Masseri returned from Jerusalem with what he had been reliably informed was a piece of the True Cross. He donated it to the Scuola di S. Giovanni, where it immediately caused a series of miracles piously recorded in the paintings.

5. Hereus Meets Ursula who Departs for Rome
6. The Dream of Ursula, in which her Martyrdom is Foretold by an Angel
7. Ursula, Hereus and the 11,000 Virgins meet Pope Cyriac
8. The Pope Travels with them all to Cologne
9. The Massacre by the Huns and the Funeral of Ursula

ROOM XXIII

Lazzaro Bastiani
S. Veneranda Enthroned
Preaching of St Antony
Giovanni Bellini
St Ursula and 4 Saints
Annunciation
Polyptych: Nativity and St Sebastian
Polyptych: St Lawrence and the Madonna
Bartolomeo Vivarini
Madonna Enthroned
Nativity
Holy Family
The Baptist
St Ambrose and Saints
Polyptych: Nativity and Saints
2 Saints
Madonna and Saints
Carlo Crivelli
Saints
Andrea da Murano
Polyptych: Sts Sebastian,

Vincent, Roch and Peter

ROOM XXIV

Titian
Presentation of the Virgin
Antonio Vivarini and Giovanni d'Alemagna
Triptych
Montagnana
Annunciation

Alexander III

There is a story that Pope Alexander III, a fugitive from the armies of the Emperor Frederick Barbarossa, slipped into Venice incognito, and spent the night in the Sotoportego della Madona (page 104) where a wooden plaque commemorates the event. The following morning he made his way to the Convent of the Carità that stood on the site of the Accademia. Here he was engaged as a servant in the kitchen, where he remained for three months before being recognized by a passing Roman prelate. On learning of their exalted guest, the Doge and the citizens made a procession to the monastery and removed him to the Ducal Palace where he received a state welcome. It is not true. Alexander arrived in Venice for his great reconciliation with Barbarossa on 10 May 1177. He was not alone, but came with his curia and was received by the Doge and the Patriarchs of Grado and of Aquileia, and conducted up the Grand Canal aboard the gilded Bucintoro, the state barge, to the patriarchal palace at S. Silvestro. Two months later, at a spot marked by a red lozenge, just inside the central archway of S. Marco (to the left), Barbarossa is said to have abased himself before Alexander, recognizing him as the True Pope and ending the long schism that had kept the Pope homeless.

S. Nicolò dei Mendicoli

The begging friars of St Nicholas have long gone, as have the poor pious women, the pinzochere, *who used to shelter under the 15thC porch built for them near the campanile. The interior has a pleasing confusion of styles.*

Angelo Raffaele

The archangel has had a church dedicated to him here since the 7thC. Five scenes from the story of him and his charge, Tobias (and his dog), were painted on the organ in the 18thC by one of the brothers Guardi. Nobody knows which.

Ca' Arian

14thC Gothic, now a school.

S. Sebastiano

In ten short years, Veronese turned the interior of this church into his monument. He started in the sacristy with a painting of the Virgin and the four Evangelists. On the ceiling he told the story of Esther, and elsewhere the martyrdom of S. Sebastiano. He is buried near the doors he painted for the organ.

Ca' Zenobio

Now an Armenian school managed by S. Lazzaro.

S. Basilio

Ghetto

This was the first Jewish Ghetto. The word comes from gettare *(to cast) because cannon were cast on this site until the work was moved to the Arsenale in 1390. Following their expulsion from Spain in 1492, many Jews came to Venice. All foreign groups were segregated, and a decree of 1516 moved the Jews on to the island of the old Ghetto Nuovo, where a nightly curfew was enforced by closed gates manned by guards whose wages were paid by those inside. They were not*

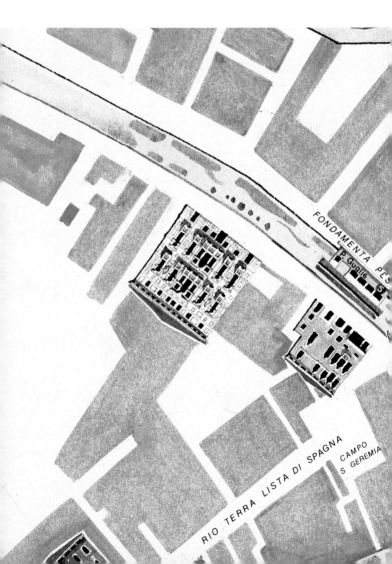

allowed to own property, but
had, instead, to pay rapacious
rents to the state, a position
so abused, that by 1735, the
whole colony went bankrupt.

Museo Israelitico
*Hours: 10.30–12.30.
Closed Saturday.*

Scuola Levantina
*Built by Longhena
(c. 1538). Adm. on request
at museum.*

Traghetto S. Marcuola

S. Leonardo
Closed.

RIO TERRÀ S. LEONARDO

S. Marcuola

Ca' Diedo

S. Fosca
With a facade of 1741.

La Maddalena
The only round church in
Venice, it was built by
Temanza (c. 1760).
Open Sundays and festivals.

Fra Paolo Sarpi
When Venice imprisoned two
priests for common crimes in
1606, refusing to hand them
over to the Pope, the city was
placed under a Papal
interdict. It was Paolo Sarpi
who devised the retort that the
Pope was master of spiritual
matters, whereas temporal

RIO TERRA D. MADDALENA

S. Marcuola

S. Stae

affairs were the preserve of
the Republic. Venice won,
but Rome did not forget.
Hired assassins left Sarpi for
dead one night on this bridge.
He recovered, to pun wryly,
in Latin, that he had
recognized the stylus ('style'/
'stiletto') of the Curia.

S. Marziale
Inside are four ceilings by
Sebastiano Ricci, and
Tintoretto's last work.

Ca' Giovanelli

Ca' Lezze

S. Felice

STRADA NUOVA

Ca' Contarini-Seriman
Now a convent school.

SS. Apostoli
*Over the altar of the 15thC
Corner chapel hangs G. B.
Tiepolo's painting of S.
Lucia, and in the chancel are
two early 14thC frescos. The
campanile is c. 1672.*

Gesuiti
*The Jesuits were never
popular in Venice. They
were organized on military
lines; in the streets, the
Pope's soldiers had to defend
themselves against abuse and
shouts that they should go and
never return. In 1609 they
did go. Doge Leonardo Donà,*

whose home is immediately behind the church, expelled them. It was 50 years before they returned, and then they engaged Domenico Rossi to rebuild the church, and to create the marvellous green and white damask hangings that everyone is delighted to discover are made of marble.

Ca' Donà delle Rose
Begun for Doge Donà, c. 1606.

Ca' Tiziano
When Titian lived here, his garden ran down to the sea.

Traghetto S. Sophia

S. Giovanni Crisostomo
*This was Mauro Coducci's
last building, and contains one
of Giovanni Bellini's last
paintings (Sts Augustine,
Christopher and Jerome). Over
the high altar hangs a work of
Sebastiano del Piombo.*

Teatro Malibran
*There has been a theatre here
since 1678, built on the ruins
of Marco Polo's home.*

Ponte Marco Polo
*This crosses into the Corte
del Milion, which is also
named for Marco Polo.*

Ca' Bembo-Boldù
On the facade is a relief of a bearded man holding a sun disc.

S. Canciano
Rebuilt in the 18thC.

Ca' Dolfin
15thC Gothic.

S. Maria dei Miracoli
It's little wonder that all young Venetians want to get married here. It is the prettiest church in the city, built in 1489 by Pietro Lombardo to house the miracle-working icon of the Madonna that sits on the altar.

A S. CANCIANO

134 S. Luca

According to James Morris, Titian's friend Pietro Aretino was buried here in 1556, after he died of laughter at an obscene joke about his own sister. Alas, both the tomb and the joke have been lost. The altarpiece is by Veronese.

Teatro Goldoni

Scuola di S. Teodoro

Now an exhibition centre. The facade is by Sardi.

S. Salvatore

The dark, gloomy interior of this 'Byzantine Revival' church soon went out of fashion, and windows were added in the 16thC (along with Sardi's Baroque facade). Vasari claims that Titian never liked the Annunciation that hangs over the third altar, yet it is emphatically inscribed 'Titianus fecit' (Titian made it).

S. Lio
Dedicated to the great reforming Pope Leo IX, whose apotheosis was painted on the ceiling by G. B. Tiepolo.

S. Maria della Fava
Fava is a broad bean, and sweets of this shape were once made and sold near by.

Ca' Veronese

The home of Paolo Veronese, the first recorded man to claim 'artistic licence' in defence of his work. The Inquisition, who questioned him about one of his paintings (see page 118), is the first recorded group to reject this defence.

Fortuny Museum

Mariano Fortuny's greatest creation was his Grecian 'Delphos' dress, a pleated cylinder of shimmering silk that clung to the body 'like perfume'. For nearly fifty years everyone wanted one, but few were rich enough, or slim enough, to wear it. Born

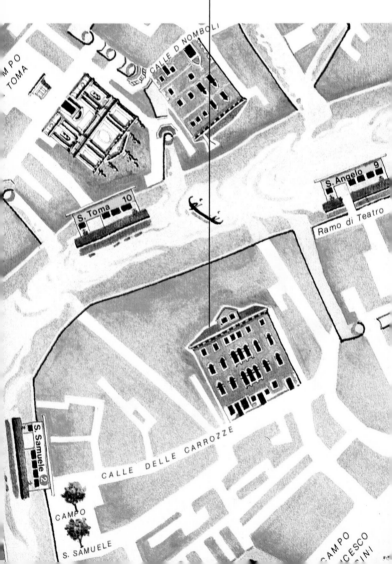

in Granada and raised in Paris, Fortuny came to Venice in 1899. This was his home and studio, where he painted, engraved, sculptured and photographed, as well as designing his famous fabrics, stage sets and lighting. It is much as he left it. Hours: 8.30–13.30. Closed Monday.

S. Benedetto

This little church contains paintings by G. B. Tiepolo, Bernardo Strozzi and Sebastiano Mazzoni. It is open in the afternoon.

RIVA DE

CALL

CAMPO MANIN

RIO TERRA D MAN IOLA

CALLE D CORTESIA

CALLE D. SPEZIER

RIO TERRA D ASSASSINI

CAMPO S. ANGELO

Ca' Loredan
Now the Institute of Arts, Letters and Science.

S. Vitale (Vidal)
Deconsecrated, it still contains Carpaccio's painting of S. Vitale on horseback. Entry is through the art gallery at the side.

S. Stefano
Rebuilt in the 15thC, this church is said to have been consecrated on six different occasions because of blood shed under its ship's-keel ceiling. Two Tintorettos and a Canova can be seen inside. The former cloisters house acolytes of the Tax Dept.

Ca' Morosini

Home of Francesco Morosini whose cannon blew up the Parthenon at Athens in 1667.

S. Maria Zobenigo

The facade contains not a single work of religious significance, but glorifies instead the supposed military exploits of Antonio Barbaro. He had in fact been dismissed for incompetence from the war in Crete by Francesco Morosini, whose house, Barbaro mischievously pointed out in his will, is within sight of this grandiose monument.

CAMPO
S. ANGELO

CAMPO
S MAURIZIO

C. 22 Marzo

Campo d.
Traghetto

S.M. del Giglio

Salu

La Fenice

Destroyed by fire in 1836, the aptly named Phoenix Theatre rose again, a perfect replica of its former 18thC self. Audiences of 1,500, seated in plush and gilt, applauded the premières of Rossini's Tancredi *and Verdi's* Rigoletto. *They booed* La Traviata *in 1853, despite their normal delight in shouting* Viva Verdi *to annoy the Austrian rulers. (His name stood for the nationalist slogan 'Vittorio Emanuele, Re d'Italia'.)*

Ca' Contarini del Bovolo

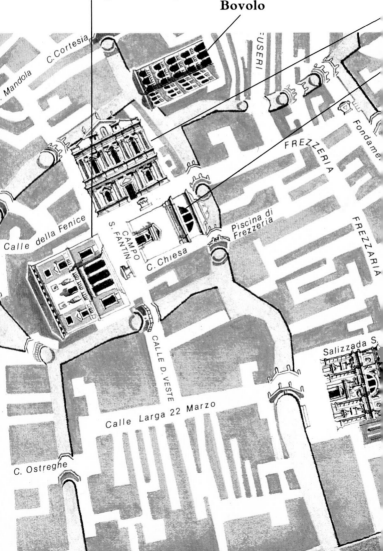

Scuola S. Girolamo

This was also known as the Scuola of the Good Death because its members had to accompany condemned prisoners to their place of execution. Since Napoleonic times it has been the Ateneo Veneto.

S. Fantin

S. Moisè

Not satisfied with the Pope's panoply of saints, the Venetians canonized Moses and built this church to him. Ruskin hated the outrageous Baroque facade by Alessandro Tremignon (c. 1668) but it is more enjoyable than that of the Bauer Grünwald Hotel.

Danieli Extension

Doge Vitale Michiel II was murdered on this spot in 1172 as he ran from the mob to the safety of S. Zaccaria. In memory, it was decreed that no stone structure should ever be built on the site, and none ever was, until 1948.

S. Zaccaria

The remains of Zaccaria, the father of John the Baptist, were the gift of the 9thC Byzantine Emperor, Leo V. The church was rebuilt in 1515, and contains one of Giovanni Bellini's finest Madonnas (2nd altar on the left; light fee).

La Pietà

The red-headed priest Antonio Vivaldi was master of music here when it was one of four Ospedale orphanages in the city. The church was built after his death by Giorgio Massari. A splendid G. B. Tiepolo ceiling can be seen if the church is open.

S. Giorgio dei Greci

Formerly the most important Greek Orthodox church in Europe, it is decorated with icons of marvellous intensity.

Icon Museum

Hours: 9.00–12.30; 15.30–17.00 or 18.00; holidays, 9.00–12.00. Closed Tuesday.

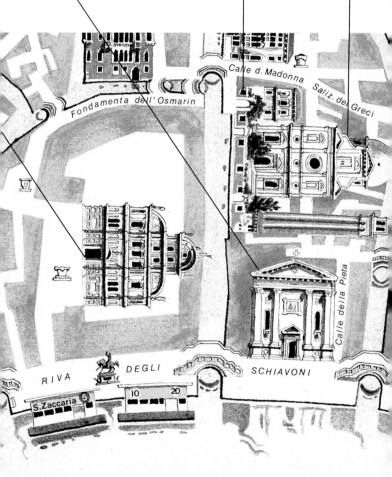

S. Martino

A Sansovino building (c. 1540) with two paintings by Girolamo Santacroce.

S. Giovanni in Bragora

Vivaldi was baptized here in 1678, surrounded by the works of Palma Giovane and Cima da Conegliano.

Arsenale

This was once the greatest naval base in the world, where a fully equipped warship could be rolled off an assembly line in 12 hours. In 1597, 100 were launched in 60 days to meet a Turkish threat to Cyprus. The rest of Europe was so impressed that

Calle d. Madonna

Saliz. dei Greci

damenta dei Furlani

Salizzada

Calle dell' Arco

S. Antonin

Salizzada del Pig

Calle della Pieta

Campo Bandiera e Moro

SCHIAVONI

145

the name of the complex, from the Arabic 'Dar sina'a' (house of construction), has passed into 14 languages. The 16,000 workforce, with their boiling pitch and tar, were Dante's inspiration for the 7th circle of Hell in the Inferno. Over the door, the lion's book is significantly closed. The word peace was not to appear in a place of war.

Naval Museum
Housed in a former naval granary. Hours: 9.00–13.00; Sat. 9.00–12.00; closed Sun.

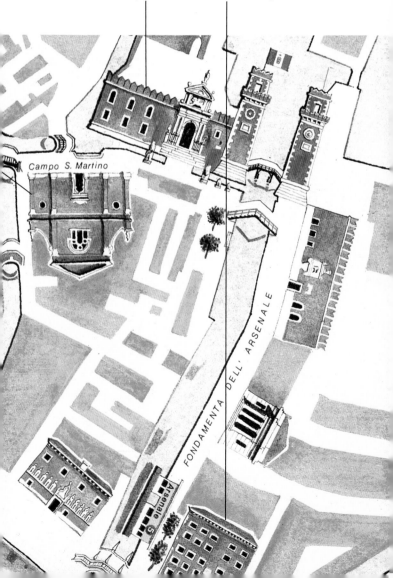

S. Lorenzo

When aristocrats thrust their daughters into Holy Orders to save money on dowries, Venetian nuns became famous, as Joseph Addison remarked, 'for the liberties they allow themselves'. At S. Lorenzo, the Patriarch of Venice had the main gate *bolted to curb the visits of masked admirers during Carnival. The noble nuns responded by setting fire to it, and burning it down. Marco Polo was buried here, but his remains were lost during rebuilding in 1592. The church opens for exhibitions.*

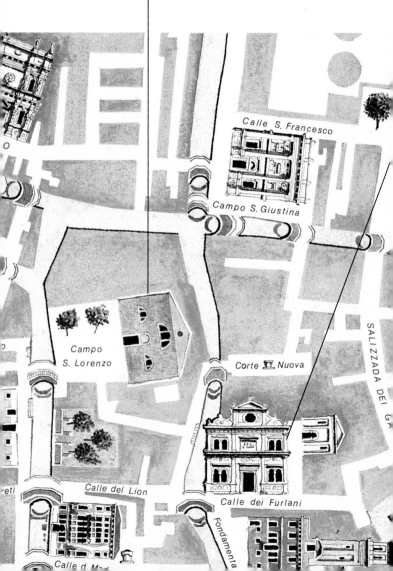

Scuola degli Schiavoni

Carpaccio decorated the hall of the Dalmatians (Schiavoni) in 1502 with three cycles of paintings, one of the great treasures of the city. Hours: 10.00–12.30; 15.30–18.00; Sun.: 10.30–12.30. Closed Mon.

S. Francesco della Vigna

It was a vineyard until it was bequeathed to the Franciscans for a convent in 1253. The church was rebuilt in 1534, with Palladio's facade added in 1572. Inside hangs a Madonna by Antonio da Negroponte, and by the door is a fine Byzantine relief.

Celestia 5

CALLE DEL CIMITERO

S. Zulian

On the facade sits Tommaso Rangone, the scholar and church benefactor. His most famous book was on how to reach the age of 120. Readership fell following his death at 80. Inside is a ceiling of the apotheosis of S. Zulian by Palma Giovane.

Ponte della Guerra

Once a site of street battles.

Ca' Querini–Stampalia

The library is on the 1st floor, and the gallery on the 2nd. Hours: 10.00–15.30; Sunday and winter: 10.00–14.30. Closed Monday.

SALIZZADA   S.   LIO

Campo S. Maria Form

C. d. Bande

CALLE DEI SPECCHIE

CALLE SP

MERC

S. Maria Formosa
In the 7thC S. Magno had a vision of a shapely (formosa) Virgin, and promptly built a church to her. Mauro Coducci rebuilt it in 1492. Bartolomeo Vivarini painted the Triptych of the Madonna and Palma Vecchio painted the altarpiece.

Ca' Donà
15thC Gothic.

Ca' Malipiero

Ca' Priuli
15thC Gothic.

S. Giovanni Nuovo
Closed.

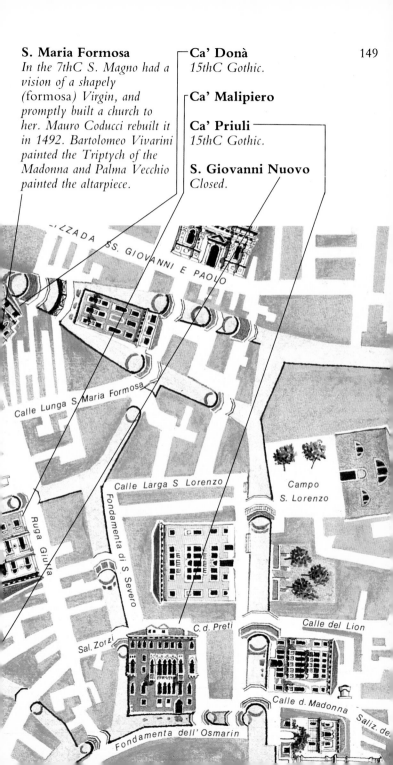

150 Colleoni Monument

When the great mercenary Bartolomeo Colleoni died in 1475, he left a fortune to the state on condition that they erected a statue to him 'outside S. Marco'. The idea was anathema – Venice never erected statues to anyone, least of all in the Piazza – but as they needed the money, it was decided that he must have meant outside the Scuola di S. Marco. The sculptor, Andrea Verrocchio, died before the work was cast, allowing Alessandro Leopardi to claim it with his signature.

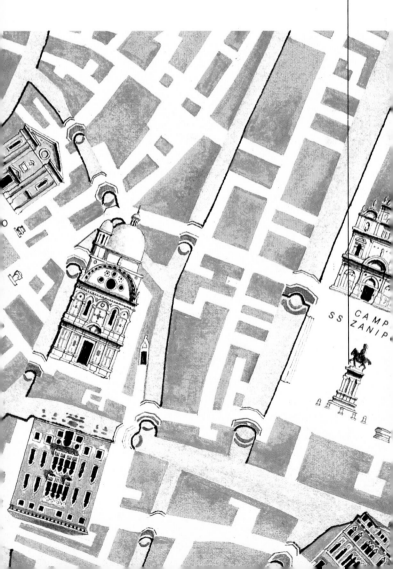

CAMP
SS ZANIP

Scuola di S. Marco
Once one of the six great fraternities, it is now a hospital.

SS. Zanipolo
See next page.

Mendicanti and Ospedaletto
William Lithgow described seeing a friar being roasted in the Piazza in 1609, for getting 15 nuns with child, 'all in one year'. Venice was awash with such orphans, and to house the girls, the four orphanages of the Ospedali were formed. These are the churches of two of them.

Ospedale 5

FONDAMENTA NUOVE

LIZZADA SS. GIOVANNI E PAOLO

SS ZANIPOLO

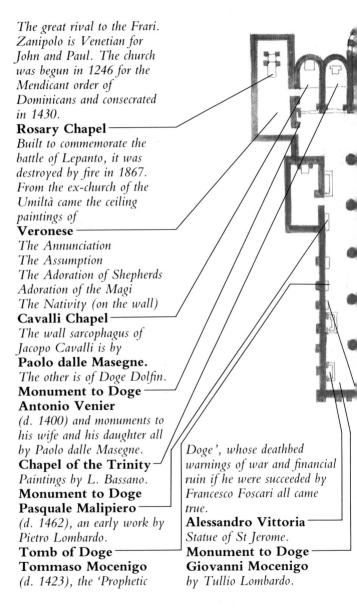

The great rival to the Frari. Zanipolo is Venetian for John and Paul. The church was begun in 1246 for the Mendicant order of Dominicans and consecrated in 1430.

Rosary Chapel
Built to commemorate the battle of Lepanto, it was destroyed by fire in 1867. From the ex-church of the Umiltà came the ceiling paintings of

Veronese
The Annunciation
The Assumption
The Adoration of Shepherds
Adoration of the Magi
The Nativity (on the wall)

Cavalli Chapel
The wall sarcophagus of Jacopo Cavalli is by
Paolo dalle Masegne.
The other is of Doge Dolfin.

Monument to Doge Antonio Venier
(d. 1400) and monuments to his wife and his daughter all by Paolo dalle Masegne.

Chapel of the Trinity
Paintings by L. Bassano.

Monument to Doge Pasquale Malipiero
(d. 1462), an early work by Pietro Lombardo.

Tomb of Doge Tommaso Mocenigo
(d. 1423), the 'Prophetic Doge', whose deathbed warnings of war and financial ruin if he were succeeded by Francesco Foscari all came true.

Alessandro Vittoria
Statue of St Jerome.

Monument to Doge Giovanni Mocenigo
by Tullio Lombardo.

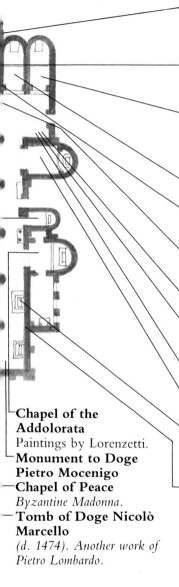

Tomb of Doge Andrea Vendramin
A Renaissance masterpiece by the Lombardo brothers

Monument to Doge Leonardo Loredan
(d. 1520)

Crucifixion Chapel Alessandro Vittoria
Virgin and St John and the monument to Sir Edward Windsor, who died in 1574.

Maddalena Chapel
Palma Giovane frescos.

Tomb of Doge Michele Morosini
(d. 1382). Dalle Masegne.

Tomb of Doge Marco Corner
(d. 1368)

Lorenzo Lotto
S. Antonino (1542).

Rocco Marconi
Christ and Sts Peter and Andrew

Alvise Vivarini
Christ Carrying the Cross

Chapel of S. Dominic
St Dominic by Piazzetta.

Giovanni Bellini
Polyptych of the life of St Vincent, and a Pietà and Annunciation. Light fee.

Bragadin Monument
Marcantonio Bragadin was flayed alive by the Turks after the fall of Famagusta in 1571. His skin is said to be in the urn beneath his bust.

Chapel of the Addolorata
Paintings by Lorenzetti.

Monument to Doge Pietro Mocenigo

Chapel of Peace
Byzantine Madonna.

Tomb of Doge Nicolò Marcello
(d. 1474). Another work of Pietro Lombardo.

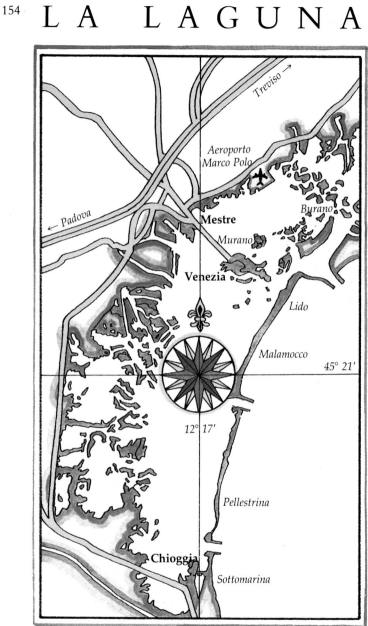

ISOLA S. MICHELE

'Here we poor folks become land-owners at last,' said the Venetian to the American W. D. Howells. But it is not true. The dead only rest in peace for ten years on S. Michele. Then they are shipped out, unless the rent is renewed, to an anonymous site on another island. A few of the famous remain. They include Igor Stravinsky and his colleague, the great impresario Diaghilev, upon whose tomb rests a pair of ballet shoes, made, as Gore Vidal points out, for a dancer with two left feet.

S. Michele in Isola
This was the first Renaissance church in Venice, designed by Mauro Coducci and completed in 1478.

Emiliana Chapel
Sailing past in 1611, Thomas Coryat 'observed a most notable thing . . . a faire Monastery of Augustine Monkes built by a rich Cortezan of Venice, whose name was Margarita Emiliana'.

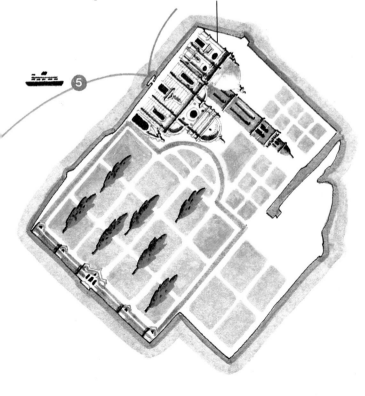

I. S. Secondo

P

34

5

9

5

20

La Gra

S ecret, judicial drown-
ings used to take place
in the Canale Orfano
in 'the silence of the night'.
Fishing was forbidden and
everyone knew why.
Napoleon swept away the
monasteries from the isles of
S. Clemente, La Grazia, and
S. Servolo, but reprieved
the Armenian order of S.
Lazzaro, which flourishes
still. Visits from 15.30 on
Thursday and Sunday.
Donations are expected.

S. Clemen

*Sacca
Sessola*

 12° 20'

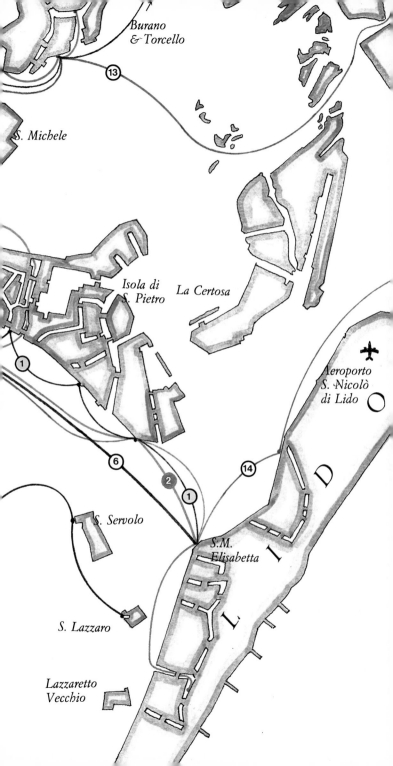

Burano
& Torcello

(13)

S. Michele

Isola di
S. Pietro

La Certosa

Aeroporto
S. Nicolò
di Lido

(1)

D

(6)

(2)

(1)

(14)

S. Servolo

S.M.
Elisabetta

L I

S. Lazzaro

L

Lazzaretto
Vecchio

GIUDECCA

These eight islands were originally called *Spinalunga*; the reason why it was changed to *Giudecca*, or *Zuecca*, as older Venetians called it, is disputed. One explanation is that there was a 13thC Jewish (*giudeo*, or *zudio*) colony here. The other is that it was a place of detention for nobles judged (*giudicato* in Italian, or *zudegà* in Venetian) guilty of lesser crimes. One known exile was Michelangelo, who came voluntarily in 1529 to stay three years.

Harry's Dolci
Harry's Bar food without Harry's Bar prices.

Mulino Stucky
An abandoned 19thC mill.

Il Redentore
In 1576, the plague claimed 50,000 lives. It wasn't until the third Sunday of July, the following year, that it was decreed to have passed. Ever since, on that day, a bridge of boats has carried a procession of thanksgiving to the church of the Redeemer, redesigned in the same year by Andrea Palladio. The festival ends with a dazzling display of fireworks, watched by everyone who can get into a boat. Inside are paintings by Veronese and Vivarini. Hours: 7.00–12.00; 15.30–19.30.

Hotel Cipriani
It has the only swimming-pool in central Venice.

Sacca Fisola

S. Eufemia

9

Le Zitelle

Another Palladian church, it gets its name ('the Maidens') from the adjoining hospice for single women.

Isola S. Giorgio was called the Isle of Cypresses (some still grow in the cloisters) before it was granted to the Benedictines for a monastery, in 982.

S. Giorgio Maggiore

This is Palladio's masterpiece, completed in 1610. The light, airy interior had a painting by Veronese, The Feast at Cana, but Napoleon removed it to the Louvre. Left behind are the works of Tintoretto, Jacopo Bassano and others.

Campanile

An elevator will lift you to the top for a spectacular view. The tower was built in 1791 by Benedetto Buratti.

Monastery

It was rescued in 1951 by the Cini Foundation, who have restored it and open it for exhibitions.

Teatro Verde

Operas and plays are often performed.

S. Nicolò

Zitelle

Redentore

MURANO

Island of glassmakers

The glass furnaces were first moved here in 1291, some say to lessen the risk of fire in Venice, others, to keep the secrets of manufacture from the prying eyes of foreigners. From earliest times, Venice held a monopoly on glass-blowing in Europe. The workers were so highly thought of that their daughters were allowed to marry into the nobility. If a master craftsman were to emigrate, he was sentenced to death *in absentia* and ducal assassins were dispatched to speed his execution. Their favoured means was the 'Venetian dagger', a fine blade of razor-sharp Murano glass, which, when plunged into the victim, would snap off at the handle, leaving but a slight scratch. Some escaped, and it is thought that the glass-works of Bohemia and Flanders were founded by dissident Muranese. By the 17thC, the monopoly was lost, but the fame endures.

SS. Maria e Donato
In 1125, a relic-raiding party returned with the remains of S. Donato, the former Bishop of Epirus. He was installed in this splendid Romanesque church, completed later in the same century. The sets of twin Roman marble columns on the facade were looted on another expedition. Inside, the mosaic pavement dates from 1140, while in the semi-dome of the apse there is a 13thC mosaic of the Virgin on a gold ground.

Museo Vetrario
On display are more than 4,000 items of glass, ranging from the Roman period to the present day, including the famous Barovia Marriage Cup of *c*. 1475, all housed in the 17thC Ca' Giustinian.

S. Pietro Martire
It contains 2 altarpieces by Giovanni Bellini, one of Doge Agostino Barbarigo being presented to the Madonna (1488), the other of the Assumption.

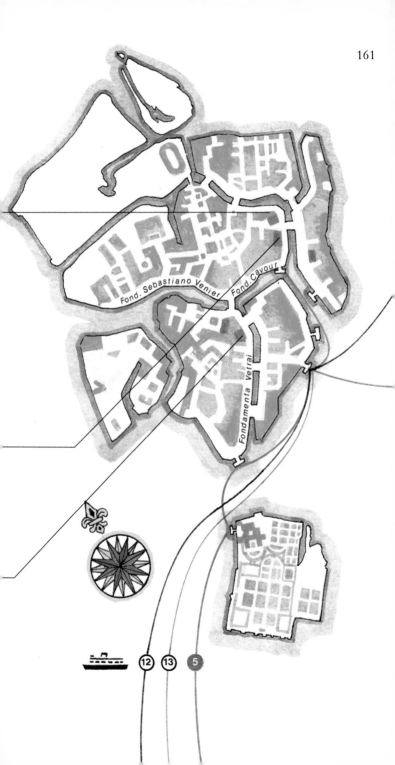

Fond. Sebastiano Venier

Fond. Cavour

Fondamenta Vetrai

12 13 5

TORCELLO & BURANO

God commanded Paolo, Bishop of Altinum, to climb a tower, and look at the stars. These would show him where to lead his flock away from the invading Lombards. The year was 639, and the place to which they were led named Torcello, after the little tower he had climbed. The flock grew to a city of 30,000, but over the centuries, silt dried up the canals and malaria wiped out the population. Today it numbers less than 100.

By contrast, Burano bustles with life. Its brightly painted houses and miniature canals make it the prettiest island in the lagoon. Once it was world-famous for its lace, but the art died of neglect after the fall of the Republic. It was revived, it is said, from the knowledge of one old lady. Traditional examples can be seen at the Lace School, but some cheaper work is imported from another island, Hong Kong.

Cathedral

With its stone shutters swinging on stone hinges, S. Maria dell'Assunta is the oldest building in the lagoon. (The foundation stone, to the left of the high altar, was laid in 639.) The cathedral contains some of the finest Byzantine mosaics in existence. The entire wall of the entrance depicts the Last Judgement. The high altar is dominated by the Madonna, all works of the 12th and 13th C. Hours: 10.00–12.30; 14.00–18.30 (winter 16.30).

Locanda Cipriani

Owned by Harry's Bar, it has some bedrooms. Closed Monday and 5 Nov. to 17 Mar. T. 730150.

Scuola dei Merletti

Lace school. Hours: 9.00–18.00. Closed Tuesday.

S. Martino

with its leaning campanile contains G. B. Tiepolo's painting of the Crucifixion.

Tre Stelle da Romano

Seafood trattoria. T. 730030.

12

LIDO DI VENEZIA

The Lido is the break-water that made Venice possible. Neither the open sea nor foreign armies could get closer. During the middle ages, crusaders camped here while the Venetians haggled over their terms of transport to the Holy Land. Since the turn of the century the invaders have been more peaceful. This is the original Lido resort, after which all the others have been named.

Palazzo del Cinema
Site of the annual Venice film festival (late August to early September).

Hôtel des Bains
The setting for both the book and the film of Thomas Mann's *Death in Venice.*

Casino
The summer casino is served by the Casino Express every half hour after 13.45.

Riveria S. Nicolo

Riviera S. M. Elisabetta

ran Viale S. M. Elisabetta

Lungomare d'Annunzio

arconi

S. Nicolò

Venetians were piqued in 1087 when the citizens of Bari, in southern Italy, plundered the remains of St Nicholas (Santa Claus) from his burial place in Lydia. Piqued enough to pretend that the theft had not taken place, despite Pope Urban II's presence in Bari for the consecration of the saint's new resting-place. Bishop Enrico sailed from Venice to Myra, and demanded that St Nicholas be handed over to him, deaf to the protests of the empty-handed custodians. The tale was told of how he fell to his knees and prayed that the relics be revealed. And lo, there was a marvellous miracle! The happy revelation ended with his triumphant return to Venice on St Nicholas's day, 1100, with a set of bones that were to be a lucrative pilgrim attraction for several centuries.

LIDO HOTELS

Byron Central Hotel
Via Bragadin 30
T.5260052; Telex 433109
April–15 Oct.
36 rooms
AMEX VISA
☆☆

Le Boulevard
Gran Viale S.M. Elisabetta 41
T.5261990; Telex 410185
Closed Jan.
45 rooms
AMEX DINERS MASTER
VISA
☆☆☆

Quattro Fontane
Via 4 Fontane 16
T.5260227; Telex 411006
17 April to 1 Oct.
70 rooms
AMEX
☆☆☆☆

Excelsior
Lungomare Marconi 41
T.5260201; Telex 410023
15 April to 20 Oct.
230 rooms
AMEX DINERS
MASTER VISA
☆☆☆☆☆

Via Sandro Gallo

Via Dardanel

Lungomare

Via Sandro Gallo

6 14 2 1

Riviera S. Nicolo

Riviera S. M. Elisabetta

Riviera

ran Viale S. M. Elisabetta

Lungomare d' Annunzio

arconi

Villa Mabapa
Riviera S. Nicolò 16
T.5260590; Telex 440170
Closed 3 Nov. to 15 March
62 rooms
AMEX DINERS MASTER VISA
☆☆☆☆

Des Bains
Lungomare Marconi 17
T.765921; Telex 410142
254 rooms
AMEX DINERS MASTER VISA
☆☆☆☆

Villa Otello
Via Lepanto 12; T.5260048
22 April to 15 Oct.
34 rooms
☆☆☆

Helvetia
Gran Viale S.M. Elisabetta
4/6
T.768403
April to Oct.
56 rooms
☆☆☆

HOTELS

La Fenice
Campiello de la Fenice 1936
Post 30124; T.5232333
Telex 411150
67 rooms
No restaurant.
☆☆☆

Saturnia–International
Calle Larga 22 Marzo 2398
Post 30124; T.708377
Telex 410355. 14thC palace
97 rooms
AMEX DINERS MASTER VISA
☆☆☆☆

Gritti Palace
Campo S. Maria Giglio
2467
Post 30124; T.794611
Telex 410125. 15thC palace
99 rooms
AMEX DINERS MASTER VISA
☆☆☆☆☆

Europa & Regina
Calle Larga 22 Marzo 2159
Post 30124; T.700477
Telex 410123
197 rooms
AMEX DINERS MASTER VISA
☆☆☆☆☆

Bauer Grünwald
Campo S. Moisè 1459
Post 30124; T.5231520
Telex 410075
214 rooms
AMEX DINERS MASTER VISA
☆☆☆☆☆

Monaco & Grand Canal
Calle Vallaresso 1325
Post 30124; T.700211
Telex 410450
75 rooms
AMEX VISA
☆☆☆☆

PIAZ
S.MA

HOTELS

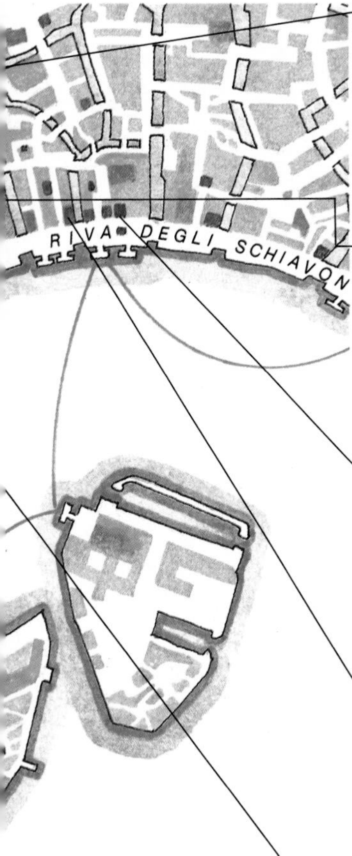

Splendid-Suisse
S. Marco-Merceria 760
Post 30124; T.700755
Telex 410590
157 rooms
AMEX DINERS MASTER VISA
☆☆☆☆

Cavalletto
Calle del Cavalletto 1107
Post 30124; T.5200955
Telex 410684
80 rooms
AMEX VISA
☆☆☆☆

Londra Palace
Riva degli Schiavoni 4171
Post 30122; T.700533
Telex 431315
69 rooms
AMEX DINERS MASTER VISA
☆☆☆☆

Danieli
Riva degli Schiavoni 4196
Post 30122; T.26480
Telex 410077
234 rooms
AMEX DINERS MASTER VISA
☆☆☆☆☆

Cipriani
Isola della Giudecca 10
Post 30123; T.707744
Telex 410162
98 rooms
AMEX DINERS MASTER VISA
☆☆☆☆☆

Luna
Calle dell' Ascensione 1243
Post 30124; T.5289840
Telex 410236
125 rooms
AMEX VISA
☆☆☆☆

HOTELS

San Cassiano
Santa Croce 2232
Post 30125; T.705477
Telex 223479 Grand Canal
35 rooms
AMEX DINERS
☆☆☆

Torino
Calle delle Ostreghe 2356
Post 30124; T.5205222
No restaurant
20 rooms
AMEX DINERS MASTER VISA
☆☆☆

Ala
Campo S. Maria del Giglio
2494
Post 30124; T.708333
Telex 410275
80 rooms
AMEX DINERS MASTER VISA
☆☆☆

Do Pozzi
Calle Larga 22 Marzo 2373
Post 30124; T.707855
35 rooms
AMEX DINERS MASTER VISA
☆☆☆

Flora
Calle Larga 22 Marzo 2283a
Post 30124; T.5205844
Small flower garden
44 rooms
AMEX DINERS MASTER VISA
☆☆☆

San Moise
San Marco 2058
Post 30124; T.703755
Telex 223534
18 rooms
NO CARDS
☆☆

San Marco
Calle dei Fabbri 877
Post 30124; T.704247
Telex 215660
60 rooms
AMEX DINERS MASTER VISA
☆☆☆

Concordia
Calle Larga S. Marco 367
Post 30124; T.5206866
Telex 411069
60 rooms
AMEX VISA
☆☆☆

Gabrielli Sandwirth
Riva degli Schiavoni 4110
Post 30122; T.5231580
Telex 410228
110 rooms
AMEX DINERS MASTER VISA
☆☆☆☆

Metropole
Riva degli Schiavoni 4149
Post 30122; T.705044
Telex 410340
64 rooms
AMEX DINERS MASTER VISA
☆☆☆☆

Panada
Calle dei Specchieri 646
Post 30124; T.5209088
Telex 410153
46 rooms
AMEX DINERS MASTER VISA
☆☆☆

Savoia & Jolanda
Riva degli Schiavoni 4187
Post 30122; T.706644
Telex 410620
56 rooms
AMEX MASTER VISA
☆☆☆

HOTELS

Brooklyn
Calle dei Fabbri 4712
Post 30124; T.5223227
12 rooms
NO CARDS
☆☆

Serenissima
Calle Goldoni 4486
Post 30124; T.700011
34 rooms
AMEX VISA
☆☆

Bonvecchiati
Calle Goldoni 4488
Post 30124; T.5285017
Telex 410560
86 rooms
AMEX MASTER
☆☆☆

San Fantin
Campiello de la Fenice
1930a
Post 30124; T.5231401
April to 10 Nov.
14 rooms
NO CARDS
☆☆

Kette
Piscina S. Moisè 2053
Post 30124; T.5222730
Telex 311877
51 rooms
AMEX DINERS MASTER VISA
☆☆☆

Ateneo
Calle Minelli 1876
Post 30124; T.700588
23 rooms
AMEX MASTER VISA
☆☆

HOTELS

Bartolmeo
S. Marco 5494
Post 30124; T.5235387
30 rooms
AMEX DINERS MASTER VISA
☆☆

Scandinavia
S. Maria Formosa 5240
Post 30122; T.5223507
27 rooms
AMEX DINERS VISA
☆☆

Montecarlo
Calle dei Specchieri 463
Post 30124; T.707144
Telex 411098
48 rooms
AMEX DINERS MASTER VISA
☆☆☆

Bisanzio
Calle della Pietà 3651
Post 30122; T.70311
40 rooms
AMEX MASTER VISA
☆☆☆

Patria & Tre Rose
Calle dei Fabbri 905
Post 30124; T.5222490
31 rooms
MASTER VISA
☆☆☆

Castello
Calle Figher Castello 4365
Post 30122; T.5230217
Telex 311879
26 rooms
AMEX DINER MASTER VISA
☆☆☆

RESTAURANTS

★Antico Martini
Campo S. Fantin 1983
T.5224121
Closed Tues. and midday
Wed.
AMEX DINERS MASTER
$$$$$+15%

Taverna la Fenice
Campiello della Fenice 1938
T.5223856
Closed Sun. and midday
Mon.
AMEX DINERS MASTER VISA
$$$$$+15%

★La Caravella
Calle Larga 22 Marzo 2397
T.708901; parchment menu
Closed Wed.
AMEX DINERS MASTER VISA
$$$$+12%

Al Giglio
Campo S. Maria de Giglio
2477
T.32368
Closed Wed.
AMEX DINERS MASTER VISA
$$$+15%

★Noemi
Calle dei Fabbri 909
T.5225238; elegant
Closed Sun. and midday
Mon.
AMEX DINERS MASTER VISA
$$$+15%

★★Harry's Bar
Calle Vallaresso 1323
T.5236797; celebrity bar
Closed Mon.
AMEX DINERS MASTER VISA
$$$$$+20%

RESTAURANTS

Città di Milano
Campiello S. Zulian 590
T.27002
Closed Mon.
AMEX DINERS MASTER VISA
$$$+12%

Do Forni
Calle dei Specchieri
457/468
T.5237729; visited by
Charles and Di
Closed Thu.
AMEX DINERS MASTER VISA
$$$$

Panada
Calle Largo S. Marco 656
T.27358
Closed Sun. evening and
Mon.
NO CARDS
$$$

Do Leoni
Riva degli Schiavoni 4175
T.25032; nouvelle cuisine
Closed midday Tues.
AMEX DINERS MASTER VISA
$$$$$

Cipriani
Isola della Giudecca 10
T.707744
AMEX DINERS MASTER VISA
$$$$$

Danieli
Riva degli Schiavoni 4196
T.5226480
AMEX DINERS MASTER VISA
$$$$$

RESTAURANTS

Al Campiello
Calle dei Fuseri 4346
T.706396
Closed Mon.
AMEX DINERS MASTER VISA
$$$+13%

Da Ivo
Calle dei Fuseri 1809
T.5285004; Tuscan
tendency
Closed Sun.
AMEX DINERS MASTER VISA
$$$+13%

La Colomba
Piscina di Frezzeria 1665
T.5221175; mostly fish
Closed Wed.
AMEX DINERS MASTER VISA
$$$+12%

Al Teatro
Campo S. Fantin 1916
T.21052; also a café/bar
Closed Mon.
AMEX DINERS MASTER VISA
$$$+12%

Da Raffaele
Fondamenta delle Ostreghe
2347
T.5232317; outdoor tables
Closed Fri.
AMEX DINERS MASTER VISA
$$$+12%

Da Bruno
Calle del Paradiso 5731
T.5221480
Closed Tue.
NO CARDS
$$+10%

Al Conte Pescaor
Piscina S. Zulian 544
T.5221483
Closed Sun. and midday
Mon.
AMEX DINERS MASTER VISA
$$$

Al Giardinetto
Salizzada Zorzi 4928
T.5285332; with a garden
Closed Sat.
AMEX DINERS VISA
$$+12%

Antico Pignolo
Calle dei Specchieri 451
T.28123; fish
Closed Tues.
AMEX DINERS MASTER VISA
$$$

Malamocco
Campiello del Vin 4650
T.27438; with a garden
Closed Fri.
NO CARDS
$$$

RESTAURANTS

Nono Risorto
Sottoportego della Croce
2337
T.27630; trattoria with a
pergola
Closed Tues.
NO CARDS
$–$$

Osteria da Fiore
Calle del Scaleter 2202
T.721308
Closed Sun., Mon.
AMEX DINERS
$$–$$$

**Antica Trattoria Poste
Vecie**
Pescaria 1608
T.721822; typical trattoria
Closed Mon. evening and
Tues.
NO CARDS
$$–$$$

La Madonna
Calle della Madonna 594
T.5223824; trattoria
Closed Wed.
NO CARDS
$$+11%

Harry's Dolci
Fondamenta S. Biagio 773
T.24844
Closed Mon.
AMEX DINERS MASTER VISA
$$–$$$

A la Vecia Cavana
Rio Terrà SS. Apostoli
4624
T.5287106
Closed Tues.
AMEX DINERS MASTER VISA
$$–$$$+12%

Fiaschetteria Toscana
S. Giovanni Crisostomo
5719
T.5285281
Closed Tues.
MASTER VISA
$$+12%

★Al Graspo de Ua
Calle dei Bombaseri 5094
T.5223647; taverna
Closed Mon., Tue.
AMEX DINERS MASTER VISA
$$$+16%

Al Pozzo
Calle dei Fabbri 1016
T.23649
Closed Mon.
NO CARDS
$$+12%

Antica Carbonera
Calle Bembo 4648
T.5225479; trattoria
Closed Tues.
AMEX DINERS MASTER VISA
$$–$$$+12%

CALENDAR

6 – 1°C

42 – 33°F

6 Days   **76** Humidity

JANUARY

Exhibitions

The new year begins with exhibitions in the countless galleries, churches and *palazzi*. The current list is found in the free publication *Un Ospite di Venezia*.

8 – 2°C

46 – 35°F

6 Days   **76** Humidity

FEBRUARY

Carnival

This is celebrated in the two weeks before Lent. Masks and costumes are worn night and day, and a variety of special entertainments are arranged all over the city.

12 – 5°C

53 – 41°F

7 Days   **68** Humidity

MARCH

Spring Casino

Towards the end of March the Casino returns to its summer location on the Lido.

Fencing

The City of Venice Cup at the Arsenale Sports Centre.

CALENDAR

17 – 10°C

62 – 49°F

9 Days   **67** Humidity

APRIL

Spring Concerts
Concerts are staged in the city's churches and theatres.

Feast of St Mark
Special services are held on the 25th, when the Pala d'Oro is exposed on the altar.

21 – 14°C

70 – 56°F

8 Days   **69** Humidity

MAY

The Vogalonga
The 'long row' is held on the Sunday after Ascension and is open to anyone wishing to row the 32 km from St Mark's to Burano and back. They start at 9.30 and return after 15.00.

25 – 17°C

76 – 63°F

8 Days   **65** Humidity

JUNE

Biennale
Every even year the Biennale International Exhibition of Modern Art is held in the permanent pavilions in the public gardens and elsewhere.

CALENDAR

27 – 19°C

81 – 66°F

7 Days   **64** Humidity

JULY

Redentore

On the 3rd Sunday, a bridge of boats is formed across the Giudecca Canal to the church of the Redentore. The festival culminates in a display of fireworks.

Festival of Dance

27 – 18°C

80 – 65°F

7 Days   **63** Humidity

AUGUST

Film Festival

The International Film Festival is held at the Palazzo del Cinema on the Lido, at the end of August and early September. Films are shown night and day for two weeks. A celebrity event.

24 – 16°C

75 – 61°F

5 Days   **64** Humidity

SEPTEMBER

Regata Storica

On the first Sunday a procession of historic boats manned by costumed oarsmen signals the beginning of the regatta.

Autumn Concerts

The season begins again.

CALENDAR

19 – 11°C

65 – 53°F

7 **68**
Days Humidity

OCTOBER

Autumn Casino

As the Lido closes, the Casino returns to Ca' Vendramin, its winter home.

Music

The symphony season begins with concerts all over the city.

12 – 17°C

53 – 44°F

8 **75**
Days Humidity

NOVEMBER

Festa della Salute

Two bridges of boats are laid across the Grand Canal, one by the Dogana and the other from Campo S. Maria del Giglio, on the 21st.

OPERA & BALLET

8 – 3°C

46 – 31°F

8 **79**
Days Humidity

DECEMBER

Opera and Ballet

The season runs through to May, with works at the Fenice and the Malibran.

Concerts

Special Christmas concerts are always arranged.

EMERGENCY!

113

POLICE

FIRE

AMBULANCE

The number is free. You will be asked which service you need.

AMBULANCE BLUE CROSS
523 0000
Mestre   98 8988

POLICE
Carabinieri
Emergency   112
Vigili Urbani   2 4063
Questura   70 3222

DOCTOR/DENTIST
See Yellow Pages or phone
Unita Sanitaria Locale
70 8811 (3493 Dorsoduro)
3 6132 (2689 Castello)

AIRLINES
Alitalia   70 0355
British Airways   70 5699
TWA   70 3219   70 3220

ROAD SERVICE
Car breakdown   116

CONSULATES
Argentina   2 7503
Austria   70 0459

EMERGENCY!

Belgium   522 4124
Brazil   70 4131
Denmark   70 6822
France   522 2392/522 4319
Germany (West)   522 5100
Great Britain   2 7207
Greece   523 7260
Guatemala   522 2532
Holland   522 5544
Liberia   522 4809
Luxembourg   522 2047
Mexico   523 7445
Monaco   522 3093
Norway (Mestre)   96 2050
Portugal   522 3446
Panama   76 6647
San Marino   70 4422
Spain   70 4510
Sweden   79 1611
Switzerland   522 5996/
70 3944
USA (Trieste)   (040)
68728

LOST PROPERTY

Airport (Marco Polo)
66 1266
Railway station   71 6122

TRAVEL INFORMATION

Airport   66 1262
Railway Station   71 5555
Harbour (Day)   70 3044
Harbour (Night)   70 5600

POST OFFICE

Fondaco dei Tedeschi
70 4143

BIBLIOGRAPHY

BATTILANA, MARILLA, *English Writers and Venice 1350–1950*, Venice, 1981

Blue Guide Venice, London, 1980

HONOUR, HUGH, *The Companion Guide to Venice*, London, 1965

KENDALL, ALAN, *Vivaldi*, London, 1978

LAURITZEN, PETER, *Palaces of Venice*, London, 1978

LIEBERMAN, RALPH, *Renaissance Architecture in Venice*, London, 1982

MORRIS, JAMES, *Venice*, London, 1960; 2nd rev. ed., London, 1983

LINKS, J. G., *Venice for Pleasure*, London, 1966

Views of Venice by Canaletto, New York, 1971

NORWICH, JOHN JULIUS, *A History of Venice*, London, 1977, 1981, 1982

McCARTHY, MARY, *Venice Observed*, London, 1956

MICHELIN GUIDE, *Italia*, current edition.

PIZZARELLO, UGO, *Boats in Venice*, Venice, 1984

VASARI, GIORGIO, *Lives of the Artists*, various editions

VILLA, GIANCARLO, *An Introduction to Venice*, Venice, 1983

VITTORIO, EUGENIO, *The Gondolier and his Gondola*, Venice, 1979

VIDAL, GORE, *Vidal in Venice*, London, 1985

ZORZI, ALVISE, *Venice: City–Republic–Empire*, London, 1983